Cyberwar
Point. Click. Destroy.

Francha Roffé Menhard

Enslow Publishers, Inc.

40 Industrial Road	PO Box 38
Box 398	Aldershot
Berkeley Heights, NJ 07922	Hants GU12 6BP
USA	UK

http://www.enslow.com

For Ken

Library of Congress Cataloging-in-Publication Data

Menhard, Francha Roffé.
    Cyberwar: point. click. destroy. / Francha Roffé Menhard.
        p. cm. — (Issues in focus)
    Includes bibliographical references and index.
    ISBN 0-7660-1591-2 (hardcover)
    1. Information warfare—Juvenile literature. 2. United
States—Defenses—Juvenile literature. 3. Computer networks—
Security measures—United States—Juvenile literature. I. Title.
II. Series: Issues in focus (Hillside, N.J.)
    U163.M397 2003
    355.3'43—dc21

Printed in the United States of America   **2002**012522

10 9 8 7 6 5 4 3 2 1

Illustration Credits: All photos are courtesy of U.S. Department
of Defense except for the following: DíAMAR Interactive Corp.:
p. 100; EyeWire Images: pp. 47, 58, 80; National Aeronautics
and Space Administration: pp. 30, 34, 70; National Archives:
p. 16; National Cryptological Museum, National Security
Agency: p. 18; courtesy of Seeds of Peace: p. 105.

Cover Illustrations: Computer circuit board and lightning from
PhotoDisc, Inc.; monitor from Hemera Technologies, Inc.; images
in monitor © Corel Corporation.

Contents

Cyberwar

September 11, 2001: Terrorists hijacked planes and crashed them into the twin towers of New York City's World Trade Center and the Pentagon in Washington, D.C. Before the bodies could be counted or the terrorists identified, "experts" around the United States began to predict that a cyberattack would be next. "Terrorists attacked our financial and political centers," security consultant Donn Parker told *USA Today*. "The logical next step is to attack our computer infrastructure."[1] For example, terrorists could make things worse by taking out New York's 911 network in a time of emergency.

The National Infrastructure Protection Center (NIPC) held emergency meetings and warned Americans that computer networks and the Internet might be next. For a cyberattack—an attack on information using computer technology—"you need one guy and a laptop," warned Michael Vatis, former director of the NIPC.[2] U.S. Senator Ron Wyden (D-Oregon) proposed a National Guard–style corps of volunteer information-technology professionals and equipment to be ready for trouble. And Senator Bob Bennett (R-Utah) introduced his own cybersecurity bill barely two weeks after the attack. President George W. Bush appointed Richard Clarke to advise him on cyber-security, to protect the nation from computer attack.

Cyberwar, the Pentagon has been warning for years, could be as crippling as a physical attack. America's enemies would use computers to take out the nation's electric power, telephone systems, air traffic control, and the Internet.

What is cyberwar? What will it look like? Who will the enemy be? How will America respond? Is cyberwar really something Americans need to worry about?

A New Kind of War

1994: The United States was under attack, but only a few people knew about it. Computers at Rome Air Development Center at Griffiss Air Base in New York were under cyberattack. By the time Air Force computer specialists discovered the attack, it had already been going on for five days.

What was going on? No one knew. But some thought it might be the beginning of a whole new kind of war—cyberwar.

For weeks, the cyberattackers made themselves at home in seven Air Force computers. They cracked

Shown is the west-facing wall of the Pentagon in Washington, D.C., following the terrorist attack on September 11, 2001. Some people feared a cyberattack would be next.

passwords and downloaded sensitive battlefield simulations. They also stole artificial intelligence research and the American Air Order of Battle—a listing of air facilities with aircraft counts and status. They used the Rome Air Development Center computers as a base for attacking other systems. Altogether, they penetrated more than one hundred computer networks, including systems at the headquarters of the North Atlantic Treaty Organization (NATO), the National Aeronautics and Space Administration (NASA), and defense contractor Lockheed.

In the past, if someone bombed an air base inside the United States, the response would have been swift and deadly. But this time it was different. This was cyberwar. Who was the attacker? No one knew. Where was the attack coming from? No one knew. What was the motive? No one knew. All anyone knew for sure was that someone had attacked the most powerful military on earth on its home soil. And there was nothing the United States could do about it.

Number One Threat to U.S. Security

The Pentagon considered the attackers the "No. 1 threat to U.S. security."[3] And the Air Force investigators could only wait for another attack to come. They could have shut the attackers out of the system, of course. But then there would have been no hope of tracking them down.

Meanwhile, someone calling himself Datastream Cowboy planted a sniffer program on the Air Force computers. Sniffers steal passwords and other data. He used the passwords to gain root access. Root access means that an attacker gains administrator privileges— complete control of a computer system. The Cowboy now had the power to copy, change, or delete information. He could crash the computer if he wanted to.

On the Trail of the Cowboy

Air Force investigators traced the intruder back through one network after another. They studied the Rome Labs network logs for clues as to the network the hacker was coming from. Then they contacted the administrator of that network, who studied the network's logs for clues. They found that the intruders had traveled through networks in Europe, South Africa, Mexico, and South America. After an intruder calling himself Kuji hacked into Goddard Space Flight Center from a computer in Latvia, a country in Eastern Europe, the Central

Intelligence Agency (CIA) became convinced that he was a member of an Eastern European spy ring.

April 15, 1994: Air Force computer investigators watched in horror as an intruder used the Rome Labs computer to attack the computers of the Korean Atomic Research Institute. Was the Institute in North or South Korea? The Air Force could not be sure. At that time, the United States was involved in tense negotiations with North Korea over that country's development of nuclear weapons. They feared North Korea would look on the attack from USAF computers as an act of war. How might North Korea's president respond? With a nuclear attack?

Finally, posing as hackers, investigators sniffed Datastream Cowboy out in an Internet chat room. The number one threat to the U.S. Air Force gave out his home phone number.

Datastream Cowboy was indeed a foreign national. Richard Price lived with his parents not far from London, England. When detectives from New Scotland Yard swooped down on his $1,200 computer and caught him in mid-hack, the sixteen-year-old dissolved into tears.

Kuji turned out to be Matthew Bevan, a twenty-one-year-old fan of the television show *X-Files*. He was convinced that unidentified flying objects and alien spacecraft are real. He was also convinced that the U.S. Air Force was hiding the truth about them. He had hacked into the Rome computers to find evidence.

What Is Cyberwar?

There is no single definition of cyberwar. In fact, experts do not even all use the same names or definitions to describe it. Synonyms include information warfare, information operations, infowar, netwar, and command-and-control warfare, to name a few. It is hard to understand cyberwar from official military definitions. These definitions sound more like gobbledygook than English.

- The official 1996 Department of Defense definition is as follows:

Military personnel work on computers while in flight. Computers allow staff to analyze combat situations and direct air support in battle. In 1994, a teenager in England hacked into Air Force computer systems.

Actions taken to achieve information superiority by affecting adversary information, information-based processes, information systems, and computer-based networks while defending one's own information, information-based processes, information systems, and computer-based networks.[4]

- The definition from the Institute for the Advanced Study of Information Warfare, a think tank that studies the military:

  The offensive and defensive use of information and information systems to deny, exploit, corrupt, or destroy, an adversary's information, information-based processes, information systems, and computer-based networks while protecting one's own. Such actions are designed to achieve advantages over military or business adversaries.[5]

Politicians and the media use colorful examples and descriptions to define cyberwar:

- President Bill Clinton, January 2000:

  Someone could hack into a computer system and potentially paralyze a company, a city or a government.[6]

- *The Times* of London, September 2001:

  The world's greatest superpower could be at the mercy of a handful of determined computer hackers paralyzing airports, markets and military systems with a few taps on a computer laptop.[7]

- Tom Gjelten, "Talk of the Nation," National Public Radio, 2001:

  Imagine warfare when the enemy is invisible, when an army can be defeated without a shot being fired. Instead a hacker or a squadron of hackers penetrates a computer system and brings it to a halt, a cyberattack. In theory, hackers could turn off electricity across a major city, shut down telephone communications, block the water supply, and halt the distribution of food. Why bother dropping a bomb on a city when you can do such massive damage to people's lives electronically?[8]

The problem with all the definitions and descriptions is that none is clear, complete, and all-inclusive. Martin Libicki, former senior fellow at the National Defense University, says that defining cyberwar is like the effort of the blind men to discover the nature of the elephant. One man touched its leg and called it a tree. Another touched its trunk and called it a rope. A third touched the tuft of the tail and called it a brush. All the men's descriptions were correct—as far as they went. But none of the men could see the whole elephant.[9]

2

Information, Technology, and War

Why is the United States suddenly at risk from this new kind of war? What changed to make war so dramatically different? What changed is the way the world relates to information.

Information has always been important to societies, both during times of peace and during times of war. For hunter-gatherers, knowing when and where animals would pass and where good food grew was important information. For farmers, knowing what to plant and when was important information.

Since the beginning of time, knowing when and where an enemy would attack could make a difference between winning and losing a battle, between life and death. When combat was hand-to-hand, leaders fought alongside their troops. They got their information firsthand. But voice commands could get lost in the noise of battle. So commanders developed other ways to communicate information. They used hand signals, but dust could hide those signals. They began to plan ahead and depend on staff meetings before battles to coordinate the movements of the troops.

As technology developed, so did weapons. Longbows, catapults, and firearms changed the way commanders led their troops. They no longer fought in the thick of battle. Instead, they stood behind the battlefield, often on a hill, and watched the whole battle unfold from a distance. Armies began to wear uniforms so that their commanders could identify them. Commanders dispatched messengers to communicate their orders to the soldiers on the battlefield.

Intercepting messengers and learning a commander's orders could be a big help to an enemy. So could sending in a false or changed message. Some ancient commanders tried to avoid interception by writing their orders on a messenger's scalp. Ancient Egyptians used carrier pigeons to deliver their messages. The Mongols of the thirteenth century used horsemen they called arrow riders to keep commanders in the field in daily communication, even if those commanders were separated by hundreds of miles. In fact, their leader, the Great Khan, knew what was going on in battle within days, even though he was often thousands of miles away. Kings of the Middle Ages used special seals to prove to their warriors that their messages were not counterfeit.

Throughout history, warriors sought faster and more efficient ways to communicate information in time of war. They also sought more effective ways to protect their own information from interception by their enemy. They developed secret messages that the enemy could not read. They used prearranged code names to identify people and places. They sent out spies and false information. They built roads and fortifications. And they applied developments in civilian technology to war.

Electric Communications

In the middle of the 1800s, inventors began experimenting with using electricity to communicate information. The newly invented telegraph used short and long tones to communicate messages across copper wires. Soon telegraph wires crisscrossed the United States. Electronic communications meant that that information could flow faster, travel farther, and be turned into secret code more securely. Within ten years, this new technology would become critical to the fighting of the Civil War.

In 1862, Congress authorized the army to seize all commercial telegraph lines in the North and to build fifteen thousand more miles of lines for military use only. President Abraham Lincoln visited the telegraph room of the War Department every day. There, cipher operators translated coded Confederate messages that had been intercepted. Cabinet officers, generals, and congressmen met to decide matters of national interest.

North and South alike knew how important information that traveled over telegraph lines was. Both sides seized telegraph offices to prevent warnings, sent false messages, and tapped the enemy's wires.

Intercepting Confederate telegrams helped the North discover what the enemy was up to. In one case, they captured contraband shipments of arms and ammunition. In another, they foiled a plot to firebomb New York hotels. Robert E. Lee's confidential telegraph operator tapped Union General Ulysses S. Grant's wires for six weeks. The information he gathered allowed him to capture over twenty-five hundred cattle intended to feed Union soldiers.

New Forms of Communication

After the Civil War, there was an explosion of new information technology. In 1876, Alexander Graham Bell and two partners patented the telephone. Almost immediately, the industrialized world began stringing telephone wire, and commercial telephone service began. Operators made manual connections at switchboards. In the 1880s, long-distance service was introduced.

In the late 1890s, the radio was perfected by Guglielmo Marconi. In 1898, he demonstrated the technology in America, sending radio messages

The new technology of the telegraph played an important role in communications during the Civil War. This Northern soldier is cutting the enemy's telegraph lines.

between Navy cruisers, the USS *New York* and USS *Massachusetts*. The British and Italian navies became Marconi's first customers. In 1912, the *Titanic* used a radio to report that it had struck an iceberg and that water was flooding the engine room.

The World Wars

In World War I, telephone communication permitted commanders to communicate information to their troops from beyond the range of enemy bullets and bombs. They rarely visited the front lines. But telephones depended on copper wires, and that meant that information systems stayed in one place. They could not be moved. Also, Germany used messengers on motorcycles to cut communication lines and disrupt the flow of information.

By 1920, some 10 million telephones were in service in the United States. Within seven years, radio waves were carrying the first transatlantic service from New York to London. Later, transatlantic calls would ride on cables laid on the bottom of the ocean. Television made its appearance at the 1939 World's Fair in New York City. NBC and CBS began programming in the early 1940s.

During World War II, armies fitted tanks, trucks, and jeeps with new wireless communications technology—two-way radios and wireless telephones. Commanders now could keep in touch with their troops in all theaters of war. But it was easy to identify and target communications vehicles, with their forest of antennas.

During World War II, in order to decode secret German information about what ships they were

This is a version of the Enigma, a code-generating machine the Germans used during World War II. British and American cryptographers were able to break the code, contributing to the Allied victory in the war.

targeting, British code breakers created the world's first working computer. The United States Army spent $500,000 to develop the world's first electronic computer, known as ENIAC. By 1943, ENIAC, which weighed over thirty tons and filled a whole room, was helping the United States and its allies to win World War II.

The Computer Revolution

The United States and its allies won World War II, but the atomic bomb that ended the war introduced a whole new threat. Within a few years, the Soviet Union, which was Communist, also had the atomic bomb. If the Soviet Union used the bomb, it could mean the total destruction of the United States. How would the American government and military know if an attack was coming? How would they communicate in the aftermath of a nuclear war? An atomic bomb would destroy direct communication links. Scientists in the

United States began to develop a top-secret spider web of computers hooked together with telephones. They hoped that this communication network could survive a nuclear war.

In the early 1960s, the Army began to think about using computers to launch nuclear weapons if the Soviet Union attacked the United States. The United States could use the communication network to deploy its own nuclear weapons after an attack, and top military commanders would still be able to communicate.

Soon research scientists doing military research began to use the system, called ARPANET, to communicate privately with the Defense Department and with each other. They also used it to share the nation's computers. Inevitably, the scientists and researchers realized that they could use ARPANET to share personal information. E-mail was born.

ARPANET remained a secret. Only a few lucky university students had access. Like the researchers, they discovered that it was good for much more than research. Their enthusiasm helped turn a strictly military and scientific network into what is now the Internet. By 1971, the number of host computers jumped from four to twenty-three. In 1973, ARPANET added its first international hosts in England and Norway. Eight years later, there were 213 hosts worldwide, with a new host being added every twenty days.[1]

The Internet

For many years, computers were rare, huge, and expensive. They were also not very powerful. Today's calculators are more powerful than the first computers. That changed in 1971, when Intel introduced the microprocessor. The microprocessor made it possible to build computers that could fit on a desktop.

In 1975, Ed Roberts invented the first personal computer. That one invention started a modern revolution. The Information Revolution is equal to the Industrial Revolution in terms of the incredible changes it has brought in communication, work, business, politics, and people's lives.

The Information Revolution has transformed the world from an industrial to an information-based society. Today, nations rely more and more on information. The Internet has made distance less important, as people began to communicate across the globe.

It was time for the Internet to grow away from its military roots. By 1986, the general public could experience the power and convenience of the Internet with Telnet, the first commercial version of the ARPANET, and Usenet, which provided public online discussion groups. University students across the country had access to the "Net."

By the mid-1980s, computers had shrunk from building-size monsters to machines that could fit on an office desktop. Businesses began to see the Internet as a way to communicate with their customers.

By 1988 the Internet was an essential tool for communications; however, it also began to create concerns about privacy and security in the digital world. New words, such as "hacker," "cracker," and "electronic break-in," were created.

In 1990, ARPANET was gone, but the Internet was alive and well. The next year, the new World Wide Web combined words, pictures, and sound on the Net. The online population exploded. By 1995, there were 26 million people online. By 2001, there were more than 500 million.[2]

The Internet has changed the world in many ways. People use e-mail along with the post office. They chat online as well as on the telephone. They can shop and bank online. Unfortunately, criminals have also moved online, using the Internet for illegal purposes. And soon, says the Department of Defense, the enemies of the United States will use the Internet to wage cyberwar.

The Faces of Cyberwar

What will cyberwar look like? No one knows for sure. There has never been a cyberwar. But the people who study war and the future have predictions.

In a cyberwar, says CIA Director George Tenet, there will be no bombs or planes. There will be no massing of armies. Cyberattackers will use technology that anybody can buy at their local computer store. Computer security experts may not know if a computer glitch is a normal problem or the beginnings of a cyberattack.[3]

Cyberattackers will strike from anywhere in the world and head home via Mexico, Korea, or Belgium. They will not leave so much as a hair or a fingerprint behind. Invisible, they will slip into a computer network and tape open a lock on a back door, in case they want to get back in easily. Tracking them will be like "tracking vapor," says Michael Vatis, first director of the National Infrastructure Protection Committee.[4] There may be no evidence at all—just a trail that leads to a dead end. How will the United States fight an unseen, unknown enemy?

Cyberenemies could use information systems to attack information and communications. Such attacks would hit affluent societies where it hurts the most—in the pocketbook. The United States is now dependent on the Internet for almost all aspects of daily life. Taking down the Internet could cripple banking, shopping, government communications, and military operations. A prolonged cyberattack could harm the national economy and threaten national security.

Cyberwar would benefit terrorists. Waging war used to require expensive weapons and an organized military. No more. Information technology has begun to spread power around. Having the biggest armies, the best intelligence, and the most expensive weapons will no longer give a nation the advantage. Terrorist groups, militias, or rogue states will be able to shut down a country's flow of information with cheap cyberweapons.

At Def Con 1995, a yearly underground hacker conference held in Las Vegas, a former American spy bragged that with just a million dollars and six hackers, he could bring America to its knees.[5] Winn Schwartau, security awareness educator, sets the price higher— around $100 million to do real damage.[6] But that amount is small change compared to the cost of one B–2 stealth bomber—over one billion dollars.[7]

Probably the scariest thing about cyberwar is that foreign cyberattackers will be able to bring war to the U.S. homeland. In the past, soldiers crossed oceans to fight America's wars while civilians stayed safe at home. The nation's roads and telephones and industries were safe, far away from the fighting.

Cyberwar would use the Internet to target

noncombatants. It would try to take down the complex networks that control oil and gas, electricity and communications. Already, cyberenemies are testing America's computer systems for vulnerabilities— weaknesses that will be a good place to launch an attack. America's borders will no longer provide protection from war.

On the bright side, some experts believe that cyberwar may be able to stop shooting wars before they start. Groups and nations may be able to use cyberspace to convince their enemies not to go to war at all. Oppressed people will be able to get their message out to convince the world that their cause is just. Public pressure could force their oppressors to loosen their grip. Other groups may be able to convince potential attackers that a war will not be worth it. Still others may be able to use the Internet to bring people and nations together in friendship and peace. This book will look at all these faces of cyberwar.

No one can be certain what the future holds—how the Information Revolution will play out and if the United States will ever really have to "fight" a cyberwar. But America's leaders take the possibility seriously. They are asking hard questions and preparing for a future cyberattack they hope will never come.

3

Attack of the Vandals

The year was 1998. The United States faced off with Saddam Hussein. The Iraqi leader had just expelled United Nations (UN) inspectors from Iraq. The inspectors had been there to make sure Hussein was not making new weapons of mass destruction. President Clinton was thinking about a military response. The United States was sending soldiers to the Persian Gulf.

Attack!

At the same time, the Air Force Computer Emergency Response Team spotted intrusions at four Navy and seven Air Force

24

systems. Dane Jasper of Sonic, an Internet service provider in Santa Rosa, California, monitored the hackers as they attacked more than eight hundred computers.[1] The cyberattackers gained root access to the networks. This meant that they could delete all the information on hard drives and could insert false data as well.

Next the hackers inserted sniffer programs to intercept passwords on some of the computers. They created back doors so they could get back into the system whenever they wanted. Finally, they destroyed log files—files that keep a record of everything that has happened on the network—to cover their tracks. The hackers went on to break into at least two hundred military Web sites.

The computer systems they broke into were not classified. Neither was the information on the Web sites. The Defense Department generally keeps classified (top secret) information on a physically separate computer network, SIPRNET, Secret Internet Protocol Router Network, which hackers cannot access through public Web servers. Still, the Defense Department was worried.

If just one worker attached a private modem to an office computer, hackers might be able to get in. The hackers could then install software to capture passwords that could let them access classified information.

In any case, the timing of the attacks was suspicious. The United States was busy mobilizing soldiers in the Persian Gulf. It looked like the hackers were targeting personnel records in an attempt to sabotage the troop buildup. And at least one attack on a Navy system came from an Internet service provider in the

United Arab Emirates. Still, no one really knew where the attack began, since smart hackers often "tunnel" through a number of systems before they reach their target.

The hackers also targeted NASA's computer systems. One of the items they found was a list of guards—and what times they patrolled various NASA installations. Was this a prelude to a physical attack on U.S. satellites that carried military communications across the globe?[2]

Questions and Some Answers

What other information had been compromised? Who were the hackers? Months after the Air Force first detected the attacks, the Defense Department still did not know.

About the same time, an official at the Massachusetts Institute of Technology contacted Dane Jasper. The official told Jasper that one of Sonic's customers had cracked a computer at the university. Jasper did a little research and identified the culprit as a customer who used the screen name "Makaveli." (Makaveli may have chosen his screen name for Machiavelli, the Italian statesman whose name is synonymous with deviousness and cruelty.)

A few days later, Air Force investigators also contacted Jasper. Another Sonic customer had broken into unclassified military computer networks. A bit more research showed that the customer went by the handle "TooShort." But were Makaveli and TooShort the crackers? Or was someone else using their accounts as a stop on the way from the real source of the attacks?

It was time to find out who the hackers were and what they were up to. For two weeks beginning February 10, Sonic technicians and FBI agents monitored Makaveli and TooShort as they surfed the Web. They "listened" in on chats with other hackers. They watched them break into sites in the United Arab Emirates, Taiwan, and Harvard University. And they learned that Makaveli had a mentor, a foreigner who called himself "Analyzer."

Jasper said:

> They were sharing resources and sharing access to systems. Analyzer would break into a system and give access to Makaveli, or Makaveli would break into a system and give access to Analyzer.
> . . . I did see instances where Analyzer would give him a name and password, meet him at a broken-in site and teach him how to do something.[3]

Analyzer said he was Makaveli's mentor. On February 3, an official at the Massachusetts Institute of Technology had told Jasper that a computer at the university had been cracked by one of Sonic's customers.

The attacks exploited a well-known vulnerability in the Solaris operating system for which a patch had been available for months, so the Department of Defense code-named the attacks Solar Sunrise.

For three weeks, defense officials tracked unauthorized activity. "After about the first week, we became convinced that it was probably hackers," Deputy Defense Secretary John Hamre said. "But, we didn't know for sure because there was an overseas element to this."[4] He was referring to the foreign mentor.

February 13: The *Defense Information and*

Electronics Report broke the story. It was time for the Department of Defense to inform the nation what was going on. The "modestly sophisticated" attacks were not connected to the crisis over UN arms inspectors in Iraq, Hamre told reporters. Nor had the attackers penetrated classified networks. In fact, the incident had "all the appearances of a game."[5] Then he let it slip that "the most organized and systematic attack the Pentagon has seen to date" was the work of two teens living in Northern California.[6]

"Two kids were able to create an awful lot of disruption in the Department of Defense," Hamre said. "We went to 24-hour shifts. We created a crisis action team. We had to go through an enormous amount of effort to protect the computer systems, to monitor them and clean them up."[7]

FBI agents raced to raid the boys' homes before they heard about themselves on the news and destroyed evidence. Agents caught TooShort red-handed. He was in the middle of hacking into a Pentagon computer. He kept typing until agents pulled him away from the computer.

TooShort and Makaveli's classmates were shocked. No one dreamed they could be mixed up in a federal crime. They were ordinary students—quiet, good kids— who loved messing with computers. They had built their high school's computer network and were always willing to help out in the computer lab.

Of course, one of the FBI's first questions was about Analyzer. Who was he? Where was he from? Makaveli did not know. He only knew that his mentor was "so good they'll never find him. . . . I don't even know who he really is. But he comes from a country where, if they were to know about him, they would just shoot him in the head."[8]

In the aftermath of the raid, both Makaveli and Analyzer gave online interviews. The first question on everyone's mind: Why did they do it? "It's power, dude," Makaveli wrote.[9] Was Analyzer afraid of getting caught? No. In fact, he challenged investigators to find him. John Vranesevich, of AntiOnline, which archives online security and hacker news, tried to trace Analyzer during his live interview. But the hacker had covered his tracks. He tunneled through thirteen different servers on his way to his destination. And he deleted log files at each stop so no one could use them to trace him. Deleting log files is a common hacker trick, but many hackers do not realize that they have left other evidence behind.

March 3, 1998: Analyzer took down the home page for NetDex Internet Inc., a Santa Rosa, California, Internet service provider. In its place he left a message taunting investigators: "This Page Has Been Hacked By Analyzer. . . . If u searching anyone u should search for me."[10]

As is often the case, Analyzer's bragging was his undoing. Within two weeks, a joint U.S.-Israeli investigation found the eighteen-year-old Israeli who called himself Analyzer. A special anti-hacker police unit questioned him and placed him under house arrest.[11]

How had three teenagers managed to hack into the computer systems of the most powerful military in the world?

At the time, the military was new at computer networking, reported Pam Hess, editor of the *Defense Information and Electronics Report*. Internet access also means that there are many points of weakness—points of unauthorized access. Second, Web security has been less than thorough. Most networks do not have round-the-clock monitoring. The security of the computer networks was the job of often poorly trained enlisted men. Many did not have the time or the skill to patch the security holes in their software. Security people who did see something suspicious had no official channel to notify their commanders.

Only some of the Air Force's security officers downloaded their network logs—a record of everything that has happened on the system—every twenty-four

Satellites in NASA's Earth Observing System will carry sensors to monitor climate change on earth. The Solar Sunrise hackers targeted NASA computers, among others.

hours and forwarded them to the Air Force Information Warfare Center at Kelly Air Force Base. There, the Automated Security Incident Measurement system looked for anything suspicious. But the system did not have an automatic alarm, so unless a human was paying attention, it was easy to miss evidence of an intrusion.

After Solar Sunrise, the Air Force tightened up computer security. "That guy doing the patches now has to answer to somebody," said Pam Hess. "Before they were just kind of putting [security advisories] on a listserv, where maybe you noticed it and maybe you didn't."[12]

"In the long run, Department of Defense will have to encrypt data that goes from one computer to the next. Before it leaves the computer, the message gets scrambled and then decoded at the other end," Hamre explained. Routine commercial transactions will be encrypted—scrambled so that outsiders cannot read it—but classified networks will have much stronger encryption.

"Another related Department of Defense goal is promoting computer literacy among the ranks," Hamre said. He noted that younger troops know a lot more about computers than the older generation. "We ought to find ways to help soldiers, sailors, airmen and Marines who have an interest in computers to become more proficient."[13]

Today, defense officials still point to Solar Sunrise when they talk about how difficult it is to know whether cyberattacks are recreational hacks or cyberattacks sponsored by another government.

4

Cyberintelligence

Information Age technology has changed the role of the spy forever. In the old days, spies risked their lives to sneak into an enemy's most secret places and take pictures of secret military documents with miniature cameras. They hid tiny dots of microfilm behind stamps or in fake coins. They left messages at dead drops—secret hiding places—for other spies to pick up. They handed their treasures off in brush-bys—apparently accidental meetings. Today, spies can copy information using a computer in the comfort of their home or office, with little personal risk.

In the old days, spies labored to turn important information into secret code.

32

Today, they can turn their information into gibberish in seconds with easy-to-use and hard-to-break encryption programs. They can hide their data in digitized photos, music files, or television signals.

Some things have not changed, however. Spies are still after the same thing: information. And, as was true fifty years ago, 90 percent of the information spies want is still available openly. Only now, that information is available in the vast library that is the Internet. What has always been more difficult is sifting through the massive amount of data to get to the valuable bits. Today, powerful computers can wade through oceans of information to identify patterns and spot warning signs of enemy activity that a human might miss.

Moonlight Maze

Later in 1998: The Department of Defense could finally stop worrying about Solar Sunrise. The Pentagon knew who the hackers were. The Justice Department was preparing the case against them.

The Defense Department had learned from the previous attacks. New cyberdefenses were in place. The Joint Task Force-Computer Network Defense war room had gone online in March. Immediately its sensors alerted government officials to yet another cyberattack on the United States. This attack, code-named Moonlight Maze, did not look to be the work of teen cybervandals, because this one was widespread and organized, said then Assistant Secretary of Defense John Hamre.[1]

These hackers were much more sophisticated than Analyzer, Makaveli, and TooShort. They were careful, and they obviously did not want to get caught. They covered their tracks using sophisticated software. They made their break-ins look like innocent Web-browsing. Meanwhile, they took over computers around the world and used them as a launchpad for their attacks. That made it hard to pinpoint the origin of the attacks.

The attackers also planted special software inside federal computers. The software notified a private Web site in Britain whenever new documents were available on the government networks. The less the hackers had to check back for new documents, the less likely they would be caught.

Computers today range in size from laptops to room-size supercomputers nearly as large as the very first computers. Shown is NASA's Cray Y 190A supercomputer in Mountain View, California.

These hackers seemed to be spies, based on the computers they targeted. They were after intelligence information. Intelligence is a key weapon in war. It is also a key weapon in efforts to keep the peace.

They transferred the equivalent of "a stack of printed copier paper three times the height of the Washington Monument," of electronic documents from Department of Defense networks to computers in Russia, said Air Force Major General Bruce Wright of the Air Intelligence Agency.[2] The hackers were especially interested in weapons research. They broke into the military's high-performance computer labs, where researchers use the world's fastest supercomputers to develop high-tech weapons of war.

They also targeted university professors working with the Defense Department. In fact, investigators found that the hackers had been at work long before the new war room spotted them. As far back as 1997, they had begun installing sniffers on university networks where the professors connected to military networks via the Internet to work on their defense projects. The hackers had sniffed out the professors' passwords and taken over the professors' accounts. They pretended to be those professors,[3] using their access to Defense Department networks to steal the log-in passwords of several hundred thousand individual users at the Department of Defense, according to the FBI.[4]

As soon as the government discovered the intrusions, the professors realized that their data was not as safe on the Internet as they had thought. They started to encrypt the information. They scrambled it into a secret code before they sent it. But no one could tell what national defense secrets were stolen before the government caught on to the hackers.

The attacks continued for six months. Then in June 1998, they stopped. Had the hackers gone on to other targets? Or had they just gotten so good that officials could no longer track them?

In September 1998, the hacks started up again. Three years later, newspapers reported that the attack was still going on. The attackers continued to find and exploit any weakness they could find in the system.

The Pentagon continues to insist that nothing classified was stolen,[5] but it is impossible to know for sure. Computer systems with classified information are not supposed to be connected to the public Internet. However, classified systems were connected, Public Broadcasting Service reporter Robert I. Cringely learned from confidential sources. Some webmasters at the Pentagon fixed it so that they could use their unclassified (non-secret) computers to access classified (secret) computers. This made their jobs easier, but it was stupid, says Cringely. The Pentagon ordered more than a hundred thousand employees to change their passwords.

Backhack

If this attack was not the work of a teen hacker on a joyride through Pentagon networks, who were the attackers? Security officials followed the attack back to its source. The backtrack did not lead to teens this time. It pointed directly at the Russians—seven Russian Internet addresses, to be exact, said James Adams, a consultant to the National Security Agency (NSA).[6] The timing of the attacks also pointed to Russia. They occurred on weekdays between 8:00 A.M. and 5:00 P.M. Moscow time—but not on Russian holidays, Adams said. Did this mean that the hackers were working in an office? Perhaps a Russian government office?[7]

Worse than that, claimed the NSA: The most sophisticated attacks came from Russian Academy of Sciences computers.[8] The 275-year-old Russian Academy of Sciences is that country's most prestigious scientific research institute. The Russian government sponsors the Academy, and the Academy works closely with Russia's top military labs. The United States did not think the Russian Academy networks were innocent waypoints for hackers from somewhere else.

Meanwhile, U.S. suspicions were confirmed by Oleg Gordievsky, the former London section head of the KGB. (The KGB was a government intelligence agency in the former Soviet Union.) At a 1998 conference on global cybercrime, he agreed that it was entirely possible that the Moonlight Maze hackers were Russian. There were probably organized groups of hackers tied to the Foreign Intelligence Service, or FSB, Russia's current spy agency, he said. Such groups had been known to hack the Web sites of enemies of Russia. "One man I know," he said, "who was caught committing a cybercrime, was given the choice of either prison or co-operation with the FSB and he went along."[9]

Russian Denial

So, were the Moonlight Maze attacks state-sponsored or simply "state-allowed"? That is, was the Russian government allowing the attacks or sponsoring and directing them? President Clinton pressed Russia for help. The Russian Academy of Sciences strongly denied that they had anything to do with Moonlight Maze. The Russian government said that they knew nothing about the attacks. As far as they knew, the telephone numbers connected to the seven Web sites were out of service.[10]

Russian denials of prior knowledge of the attacks did not impress former NSA consultant James Adams. He told Congress in 2000 that he believed "the information was shipped over the Internet to Moscow for sale to the highest bidder."[11]

Boris Labusov, spokesman for the FSB, was outraged at the accusation—and not because Russian hackers would not spy for the state. Russian spies, he said, would have been too clever to allow themselves to be traced. "Do you think Russian special services are so stupid as to engage in such activities directly from Moscow?" he demanded. "For decades everybody has written about how clever the KGB and Soviet intelligence are. Why should one think we suddenly became less clever in the last few years?"

Labusov pointed out the obvious: that the hackers could be anywhere. It is not uncommon for hackers to tunnel through any number of countries to reach their target. "A web server is a public service," he said. "Anybody can connect."[12]

The Cuckoo's Egg

The United States could not prove that the Russian government was behind the attacks. But if it was, it would not be the first time. Between 1986 and 1989, West German hackers broke into the computer network at Lawrence Livermore Laboratories at the University of California–Berkeley. They also compromised military, scientific, and industry computers in the United States, Western Europe, and Japan. They sold the booty they obtained—passwords, programs, and other intelligence data—to Soviet KGB spies.

1986: No one would have noticed if not for Clifford Stoll. The ex-hippie astrophysicist had just started his job as systems manager of the University of California–Berkeley Livermore Laboratories computer network. A seventy-five-cent billing error alerted him to the presence of an electronic intruder trying to use the network without paying.

Stoll could have shut the hacker out of the system, but he did not. He thought he could learn more by letting him continue to use the system. He wrote a special program that recorded the hacker's every keystroke.

The hacker worked his way through the networks that link U.S. military and industrial computers all over the world, fishing for sensitive military information.[13] "This guy broke into Air Force bases and computers all across the country, and nobody knew it," Stoll told *People* magazine.[14]

For ten months, Stoll tried to track the hacker back to his origin. The calls were coming into the Berkeley computer, he learned, via a data carrier named Tymnet. A university computer in Bremen, West Germany, was linking to Tymnet. The hacker was using a computer and modem to connect to the Bremen university. But where was the hacker? He never stayed connected long enough for Stoll to trace.

Stoll set up a sting. He loaded a file of bogus information on President Ronald Reagan's Strategic Defense Initiative (nicknamed "Star Wars") on the Berkeley network. It took the hacker more than an hour to download the phony data. That was long enough to track the hacker back to his apartment in Hanover, Germany.

March 1989: German authorities arrested Markus

Hess, a twenty-five-year-old programmer, and charged him with spying for the Soviet Union.[15]

Cyberespionage

The United States also uses cyberspies. As early as the 1980s, the NSA and CIA began scooping up classified information from the computers of other nations, a former senior government computer expert told *Time* magazine. About the same time, the agencies began to experiment with using viruses to disrupt other nations' computers.[16]

April 2001: Russian newspaper *Moskovsky Komsomolets* reported that the U.S. intelligence officials at the embassy in Moscow had attempted to recruit a Russian hacker known as Verse.[17]

Verse's job was to hack into key Russian networks. He would also write computer programs that would find and download databases of interest to the United States. He would destroy other files. Finally, he was to recruit other hackers to help him. But Verse decided not to spy for the United States. Instead, he went to the FSB and told them all about the plot.

In the ongoing cyberwar, cyberespionage is perhaps the most threatening thing. Spies around the world will continue to exploit the Internet as a spy tool. Internet spying is anonymous. It is cheaper than traditional espionage. Cyberspies are less likely to get caught than spies who physically steal information.

The Moonlight Maze cyberattacks did not breach any classified computers, and they did not damage any computers. Rather, the hackers "vacuumed up vast amounts of publicly available data" from Department of Defense, government, university, and private-sector computer networks, according to Senator Bob Bennett. But scooping up data that is available to the public can hardly be considered spying. So what is the problem? Bennett worries that the hackers burrowed into places security officials do not know about and are still vacuuming up sensitive, but not classified, information.[18]

Adding Layers of Protection

If anything good came out of Moonlight Maze, it was that the government finally moved to protect sensitive information. Before 1998, hackers could worm their way through thousands of "back-door" connection points around the globe and into sensitive government computers. No more, said Arthur L. Money, assistant secretary of defense. From now on, public access to NIPRNET (Non-Classified Internet Protocol Router Network), the Pentagon's main unclassified computer system, would be routed through eight large electronic gateways that would be easier to monitor.

Spies will continue to tromp through military and industrial computer networks because they can. Insiders and careless network users make cyberespionage possible. Careless users create unauthorized gateways from unclassified to classified computers. For example, workers sometimes attach personal modems to their classified systems. This provides an unlocked door for hackers. Even former CIA director John Deutsch put sensitive information at risk when he downloaded classified documents onto his unsecured home computer.[19]

1999: The Department of Defense began to discuss creating a third network just for military and

A first lieutenant in the Air Force monitors her computer screen. After the incursions of Moonlight Maze in 1998, the military and other government bodies tightened up computer security.

government information and communications.[20] After the attacks on the World Trade Center in September 2001, the government again began to discuss the issue. However, a third network would be very expensive. And the government continues to have a hard time keeping the best computer experts, when they can find jobs that pay so much better in private business.

A third network may be worthwhile, but as convicted KGB spy John Walker noted after his arrest back in 1985, defenses designed to protect against enemies from the outside will not protect the nation against traitors within.[21] As in the past, digital spy agencies will have to keep their eyes open for moles who would use information technology to sell America's secrets to the highest bidder.

5

Taking Down the Digital Community

Traditional bank robbers wear masks and carry guns. They sometimes leave their fingerprints behind and their images on security cameras. Traditional blackmailers leave a real paper trail or phone records for law enforcement to follow.

Cybercriminals are harder to identify and follow. They use a mouse and modem instead of masks and guns.

In the Information Age, computer networks keep track of credit card numbers, ATM card personal identification codes, bank transfers, and stock sales. Because of this, financial criminals have turned to the Internet. Any economy depends on the

confidence of the people who rely on it. Attacks—
physical or cyber—on the nation's businesses and
financial institutions can threaten consumer confidence. Of course, financial loss hurts businesses, but
loss of confidence hurts even more. In 2002, some 70
percent of businesses did not report cybercrime for fear
of bad publicity and the loss of confidence bad publicity
will bring. In previous years, as many as 84 percent did
not report cyberattacks.[1]

Cyberheist

1994: The Cold War was over, and Russia's economy
was in chaos. Vladimir Levin, a brilliant biotechnology
student, found a dead-end job writing software for an
accounting company in St. Petersburg, Russia. His
paycheck was so tiny, Levin could barely afford to live.

Then Levin got an idea. He would rob a bank. But
he would not try to pull off the old-fashioned kind of
bank robbery. He would not need a ski mask, gun, or
getaway car. Instead, he would use his slow, cheap
computer for the job. Levin targeted Citibank, one of
the world's largest banks. No one knows how he got the
employee computer codes and passwords he needed to
break into the bank's system.

Levin's first transfer on June 30 was $143,800.
Nobody noticed. When bank managers finally did
notice, the cyberthief had already made nineteen illegal
transfers and made off with some $10 million.

For a while, the bank allowed the thief to continue
to transfer money, in hopes of tracking him down.
Meanwhile, the FBI started investigating the telephone
lines the hacker had used to break into Citibank
computers. Citibank and the FBI could monitor the

thief as he moved cash out of Citibank and into accounts at banks around the world, but they had no idea where the hacker was. They could not track him back through the international maze of networks he used.

Takedown

Then the calls began coming in from clients and other banks. In August 1994, a Buenos Aires, Argentina, investment company discovered that almost $200,000 had disappeared from its Citibank account overnight.[2] A bank in San Francisco thought that one of their accounts looked suspicious. The FBI investigated and arrested Ekaterina Korolkova as she tried to withdraw money from the account. She pointed the finger at her husband, Evgueni, and he told them about their co-conspirator, Vladimir Levin. Another illegal transfer led the FBI to another member of the conspiracy, Russian Vladimir Voronin. Dutch police arrested him as he tried to withdraw more than $1 million from a bank in Rotterdam, the Netherlands. He also pointed the finger at Levin.[3]

In September, the FBI and the Organized Crime Division of the St. Petersburg police broke into Levin's workplace. There they found the evidence they needed. But it was not until March 1995 that British police arrested Levin at a London airport. Levin fought extradition to the United States for almost three years, but he lost his case. In 1997, sandwiched between two U.S. marshals, he flew to New York. Under a plea agreement, Levin was sentenced to thirty-six months in prison and ordered to pay a $250,000 fine, the amount of the stolen money Citibank was unable to recover.[4]

Cybercrime

The Citibank cyberheist is the only documented case of online bank robbery to date. But criminals will always follow the money, and they will follow it into cyberspace. Criminals of all kinds—petty thieves, extortionists, scam artists, embezzlers, and industrial spies—will continue to come up with new ways to exploit holes in the financial system, physical or electronic.

Many fear that the Citibank cyberheist is just one example of the kind of chaos a dedicated enemy could cause. The world and the nation's "very reliance on computer networks . . . creates a vulnerability that a determined opponent . . . could exploit," Dan Kuehl told Congress. America's enemies could use the hacker tools to "generate truly damaging interruptions to the national economy."[5]

People have to be confident that their money is safe and available. High-profile cyberassault on banks, brokerages, credit card companies, or Wall Street would damage public confidence and have a negative impact on the well-being of the nation.

DDoS Attacks

Commerce depends on public confidence as well. Americans expect their stores to be open at predictable times. They expect stores to have the expected products available, as well. E-commerce—cyberstores and services—have the added burden of keeping customers' information confidential. A cyberattack that compromises availability or confidentiality can affect more than just the businesses that are attacked. The resulting

In a DDoS (distributed denial of service) attack, hackers tie up Web sites so that other users cannot log on to their favorite sites.

publicity and loss of confidence can undermine all of e-commerce.

In February 2000, distributed denial of service (DDoS) attacks shut down Yahoo!, CNN, Buy.com, and other high-profile Internet sites. The attacks shook public confidence in the nation's new cybereconomy. To carry out the DDoS attack, hackers unleashed an electronic avalanche of fake requests for information. These requests overwhelmed Yahoo!, Amazon, CNN, and other sites, much as pranksters can tie up someone's telephone by repeatedly calling his or her phone number. No one else can call in. In the DDoS attacks, the result was similar. Web surfers could not log on to some of their favorite Web sites for up to three hours.

Cyberattacks, the media reported, had cost the companies up to $1.2 billion,[6] and future attacks could cripple e-commerce and destroy the U.S. economy. Dan Rather called the attacks "the crime of the new century" on national television news.[7] Attorney General Janet Reno promised to do everything she could to keep the Internet "a safe place to do business," and requested $37 million to protect against electronic attacks.[8] The FBI began a massive worldwide hunt for the hackers. President Clinton cleared his schedule to hold a Web summit to address the threat.

But the attacks were mild, said Fred Cohen, a leading computer security expert at Sandia National Laboratories. The attacks did not compromise private information or corrupt records. All they did was keep people from accessing a few Web sites for several hours.[9] All they did was cause some inconvenience. The same thing happens during storms and earthquakes: Power failures keep people off their computers. But people are used to storms and earthquakes. They do not worry that the outages storms cause will cripple the U.S. economy. They are confident that things will soon be back to normal.

The February 2000 cyberattacks did shake people's confidence, and the loss of confidence surely helped drive up stock prices of some electronic security companies 60 percent in the three days after the attacks.[10] The lack of confidence may have also hurt technology stocks, which plunged in 2000.[11]

Crime, Not War

Companies that use phone lines or the Internet to conduct business will continue to be the target of pranksters, thieves, and extortionists. Pranks, robbery, and extortion are not new, and they are not war. They are crimes, as they have always been. They only look new because they are taking place in cyberspace.

The threat of economic cybercrime will remain as long as business fails to pay serious attention to basic network security. In November 2001, for example, two

British university students revealed that they had hacked into the IBM computer that protects electronic financial transactions. Bank employees could find out the personal identification numbers that protect customers' ATM cards. "A crooked bank manager could duplicate our work on a Monday and be off to Bermuda by Wednesday afternoon," one of the students said.[12] An IBM spokeswoman disagreed. "Normal bank practice and procedure would prevent any possibility of launching such an attack," she said.[13]

The economic system will continue to become more dependent on networked computer systems. Computer students will always find holes in the networks that support business and the economy, and hackers will continue to exploit those holes. Financial institutions and businesses must pay attention to security. They must take threats seriously and be prepared for them.

The Love Bug

April 2000: The Love Bug virus hit computer networks worldwide. This virus came in an e-mail with the subject, "ILOVEYOU." The body of the e-mail read, "kindly check the attached LOVELETTER coming from me." When people opened the attached file, "LOVE-LETTER-FOR-YOU.TXT.vbs," it overwrote files on the infected computer. It also sent a duplicate of the deadly e-mail to all e-mail addresses in the computer's Microsoft Outlook address book. Many people who would never open an attachment from an unknown user were not at all suspicious of a love letter coming from someone they knew.

Experts estimated that the economic damage would reach anywhere from $2.61 billion[14] to $10 billion.[15]

The virus was estimated to have hit some 40 to 50 percent of companies worldwide.[16]

For Ford Motor Company, the Love Bug turned out not to be very disruptive at all. Early on, Ford shut down its exchange servers and prevented the spread of the virus, company spokesman Jim Yost said. Some people were inconvenienced. They could not send e-mails for a day. But Ford "maintained our other communications—voice, telephone, fax," Yost said. "We lost no production. We lost no sales. We had no disruption to our production operations."[17]

How did Ford get off so easy? The company planned ahead. "We have our mail system totally separated from our applications and our e-mail systems from our customer bases," Yost explained. "We scan incoming e-mail."[18] Ford also protects its computer systems on many levels.

Ford will continue to take security seriously. Its security experts will scan for the threats they know about and to try to detect where future threats may come from. The company will also continue to provide a way for individual employees to identify and report computer security problems.

Not all companies are like Ford, but they should be. Just as it is up to companies to lock their doors and hire guards to protect their physical assets, it is up to computer users to take the necessary steps to protect their cyberassets. Only by paying attention to cyber-security can companies protect themselves and the nation from the threat of economic cyberattack.

6

Cyberterrorism

In the past, terrorism seemed far from home. In 1998, a car bomb exploded in the center of a crowd in Omagh, Northern Ireland, killing twenty-nine, including eleven children. In 1986, Maoist Shining Path guerrillas bombed a train in Peru, killing eight. In 1972, Palestinian terrorists massacred eleven Israeli athletes at the Olympic games in Munich, Germany.

Even when terrorism touched the United States, it happened overseas. In Yemen, suicide bombers attacked the USS *Cole* in September 2000, killing seventeen American sailors. In Kenya and Tanzania, near-simultaneous bombings of U.S.

embassies killed more than three hundred in 1998. And in 1983, the bombing of U.S. military barracks in Lebanon killed 241 Marines. But those terrorist acts seemed far away and random. Soon they slipped from the front page of newspapers. The fear passed, and the memory faded from the national consciousness.

But terrorism has been coming closer to home. In 1993, a truck bomb in the parking garage under the World Trade Center in New York City exploded, killing six people. In 1995, Timothy McVeigh blew up the Murrah Federal Building in Oklahoma City. The death toll: 168. But there were only those two incidents. For the most part, Americans felt safe.

Before the September 2001 attacks, it was easy to use the word "terrorism" carelessly. It was easy to apply the label "terrorism" to hacking, crime, or even political speech. Today, sadly, Americans know what real terrorism is. The unforgettable image of passenger planes flying into the towers of New York City's World Trade Center gives new meaning to the U.S. Department of State's definition of terrorism: the "premeditated, politically motivated violence perpetrated against noncombatant targets by subnational groups or clandestine agents."[1]

Terrorism in Cyberspace

Barry Collin, a senior research fellow at the Institute for Security and Intelligence at Stanford University, California, was the first person to use the word "cyberterrorism." His definition: "hacking with a body count." Collin said:

> Like conventional terrorists, cyberterrorists are out for blood. They try to do things like break

into subway computer systems to cause a collision or use computers to tamper with power grids or food processing. However, unlike suicide bombers and roof-top snipers, cyberterrorists attack from the comfort of home and can be in more than one place at a time through cyberspace.[2]

For Mark Pollitt, a special agent for the FBI, cyberterrorism is the "premeditated, politically motivated attack against information, computer systems, computer programs, and data which result in violence against noncombatant targets by subnational groups or clandestine agents."[3]

An air traffic controller guides strike aircraft into and out of Iraq in 1998. Within the United States, soldiers travel in skies controlled by civilian air traffic control systems. A cyberattack on these systems could be disastrous.

Fear Factor

According to Arnaud de Borchgrave of the U.S. Center for Strategic and International Studies:

> Tomorrow's high-tech terrorists are plotting attacks with ones and zeros, at a place where we are most vulnerable—namely the point at which the "physical" and the "virtual" worlds converge, the place where we live and function and the place in which computer programs function and data moves.[4]

There is no physical evidence. The terrorist could be halfway around the world. It is a low-budget form of attack. Terrorists do not have to make or transport bombs.

Barry Collin described a cyberterrorist attack in which hackers would

> remotely access the processing control systems of a cereal manufacturer, change the levels of iron supplement, and sicken and kill the children of a nation enjoying their food. . . . The potential loss of life is unfathomable. . . . These examples are not science fiction. All of these scenarios can be executed today.[5]

Cyberterrorism?

It may be true that terrorists can carry out devastating cyberattacks today, but they have not done so yet. So far, the acts that governments and the media have publicized do not even come close to the classic definition of cyberterrorism. In Australia alone, officials reported fifteen thousand cyberterrorist attacks in 2001, up from ten thousand in 2000.[6] What were these fifteen thousand attacks? Certainly not the kind of thing Collin described. Rather, they include every-thing from making threats online[7] to everyday hacker bragging,[8] from digital joyrides through poorly protected government computers[9] to causing electronic traffic jams on Yahoo! and other online businesses,[10] from hacking Web sites[11] to spreading e-mails about killer bananas.[12]

All these attacks involved the Internet. Most of them were crimes. But they were not terrorism. Attacks that disrupt nonessential services or that are mainly a costly nuisance do not qualify as cyberterrorism, says Dorothy Denning, professor of computer technology at Georgetown University.[13] Terrorism, by definition, carries a body count. Not even the most serious of these incidents caused a single death.

Cyberterror: Not Yet

The FBI's Pollitt says that real cyberterrorism—not rumors of killer bananas—does not *at present* pose a significant risk. That is because there are people behind the computers a terrorist would attack. And Pollitt believes that people will notice the warning signs of a cyberterrorist attack.

In the cereal factory, for example, to kill a child, cyberterrorists would have to up the dose of iron to between five and ten grams. Most cereal has less than one-half milligram of iron per serving. A lethal dose is ten thousand to twenty thousand times higher.[14] Certainly someone would notice the change. The assembly line would run out of iron early. If the cereal did reach the market, it would taste strange.

In the air traffic control tower and in airplanes, as well, there are people behind the computers. Air traffic controllers are professionals who are trained to notice irregularities and correct problems. Pilots are trained professionals, too. While flying, they regularly catch air traffic control errors, and they can fly safely with no air traffic control at all.

Terrorists in Cyberspace

So far, terrorists have not used the Internet to cause violence or serious economic or social harm. What terrorists have done, however, is use cyberspace to facilitate traditional forms of terrorism, Denning says. They put up Web sites to spread their message of hate and to recruit new members. They use Web sites and e-mail to communicate with each other and to coordinate action.

For example, Palestinian activists have used chat rooms and e-mail to plan terrorist operations—such as suicide bombings—against Israel.[15] And in the United States, an anti-abortion group used the Web to publish a hit list of doctors "guilty of crimes against humanity." After the murder of one of the doctors, Web site owners crossed his name off the list.[16]

1996: Terrorist Osama bin Laden's Afghanistan headquarters had a high-tech communications network complete with e-mail, electronic bulletin boards, and access to the World Wide Web.[17] This is amazing, considering that there were just over thirty thousand telephone lines in the entire country of Afghanistan as late as 1998 and no Internet provider.[18] In 1998, bin Laden discovered that the CIA was listening to communications on his satellite phone and began relying more on e-mail and the Internet. His terrorists sometimes posted messages at one of the Web's 2 billion pages.

Other times they disguised their messages as spam—unwanted e-mail advertising—or hid their messages in one of the Web's 28 billion image files.

Hiding messages in an image is not difficult, according to Dorothy Denning:

> You select an image file. You type your covert message in another file, then combine and encrypt them with the software program. It will ask you for a password, which is the encryption key. Then somebody else with the password can uncover the message, but it won't be apparent to anybody else.[19]

Shown is a group of terrorist camps in Afghanistan after military strikes in 1998. Terrorists used the Internet and e-mail despite the scarcity of services in that country.

Even an innocent picture like this can hide secret messages to be decoded.

After the September 2001 terror attacks on the World Trade Center and Pentagon, terrorist hunters got a lucky break. They recovered some of the terrorists' e-mails. Finding the files gave the FBI new insight into bin Laden's organization, said Edward Turzansky, a political science professor who has worked with the Department of Defense. "Think of intelligence as a huge puzzle," he said. "We were sitting there with 1,500 pieces, not knowing how to proceed. Now somebody's handed us the box with the picture on the front."[20]

Cyberterrorism: Unlikely

Are America's enemies seeking to use cyberterrorism, either alone or in conjunction with acts of physical violence?

No, wrote the Center for the Study of Terrorism and Irregular Warfare at the Naval Postgraduate School in Monterey, California, in its 1999 report, "Cyberterror: Prospects and Implications." Terrorists do not have the ability to mount anything more than annoying hacks.[21]

No, says the Department of State, which since 1995 has published "Patterns of Global Terrorism." None of its reports includes a single instance of cyber-terrorism.

No, says Dorothy Denning, because terrorists cannot predict how a cyberattack would turn out. Old terrorist methods have worked fine for hundreds of years. Why should terrorists try new ones? Furthermore, unless people are injured, there is less drama and emotional appeal. Cyberterror may be too quiet. Terrorists like to see things go boom. For now, Denning says, "the truck bomb poses a much greater threat than the logic bomb."[22] If cyberterrorism is the way of the future, it is at least a few years away, says Denning. At present, there is little concrete evidence that anyone is preparing to use the Internet for terrorism.[23] But the next generation of terrorists is growing up in a digital world. They may be much more comfortable in cyberspace and may turn to cyberter-rorism as governments improve defenses against traditional terrorism.

7

Sum of All Fears: Infrastructure Warfare

The Constitution of the United States gives the federal government the responsibility of protecting the nation from attack. Throughout American history, the federal government has assigned that job largely to the military. For the federal government and for the military, protecting the United States from attack used to mean protecting the nation's physical infrastructure—its borders, airports, bridges, highways, dams, power plants, weapons facilities, and military and government buildings.

Today it also means protecting the nation's information infrastructure. This includes the physical and cyber systems

60

that allow the government and the economy to function. It is made up of computer networks that control the nation's telephones, e-mail, power companies, air traffic, banking, the stock markets, water, and emergency systems. All these systems are interconnected. That makes them more efficient, but it also makes them easier to attack.

No country has benefited more from network technology than the United States. At the same time, no country is more dependent on it. The government, military, industry, and individuals depend on having the information infrastructure up and running in order to carry out the activities of their daily lives. An enemy would only have to disrupt America's information infrastructure to create great confusion and hardship.

It is the military's job to protect this vast infrastructure, but the law does not give the military authority to protect commercial phone lines, the electrical power grid, and vast, vital databases. And the military is as dependent on the information infrastructure as the rest of American society.[1]

Ninety-five percent of military communications use civilian phone networks and the civilian Internet. U.S. military bases rely on private companies for their electricity, natural gas, and heating oil. The Pentagon relies on the federal banking network to pay salaries and make purchases. Soldiers travel in skies and on rails controlled by civilian air traffic and railroad control systems. "In short," says Neil Munro, author of *The Quick and the Dead: Electronic Combat and Modern War*, "if the civilian computers stopped working, America's armed forces couldn't eat, talk, move or shoot."[2]

That is why today, no country is more vulnerable to

A combat weather team forecaster aligns a satellite dish. Some fear that a cyberattack could disrupt satellite communications.

cyberattack. America's enemies know that they can strike at the information infrastructure of the nation more easily, more cheaply, and with less danger of reprisal than if they attacked the physical infrastructure. The United States must be prepared.

Preparing for an "Electronic Pearl Harbor"

December 7, 1941: The Japanese Imperial Navy caught the United States unprepared. On a quiet Sunday morning, Japan launched a surprise attack on Pearl Harbor, destroying more than 180 American planes and five ships, and damaging many more vessels. The nation was in shock. The next day, President Franklin D. Roosevelt declared war.

For the past ten years, the Department of Defense has been worrying that an "electronic Pearl Harbor" could take the nation by surprise. In order to be better prepared for this worst-case scenario, they have to predict what an electronic Pearl Harbor might look like. They used war games to help them.

In 1996, RAND, a think tank that has worked with

the military since the end of World War II, sponsored an exercise to help the Defense Advanced Research Projects Agency with its predictions. "The Day After . . . in Cyberspace," summed up the nation's worst fears of what cyberwar might look like. Participants from the military, government, and private industry had to figure out what the United States should do if a cyberwar actually happened.

"The Day After . . . in Cyberspace"

In this fictional scenario, Iran had been demanding that other oil-producing nations cut production by 20 percent. Cutting production would increase demand for oil and drive up prices. Iran would profit. The other nations refused, and Iran prepared for war. Iran and Saudi Arabia tangled on the sea and in the air.

In Washington, D.C., high military officials, CIA and FBI security specialists, foreign policy analysts, and White House staffers met around the clock to address the latest crisis. Outside the White House and across the country, activists demonstrated, demanding that the United States stay out of the conflict.

Within twelve hours, the telephone system in Texas suddenly failed. Thousands of incoming calls paralyzed switchboards at Ft. Lewis, Washington. A Metroliner passenger train heading for New York crashed headlong into a freight train. As CNN reported on the crash, it lost its signal for twelve minutes. In Los Angeles, air traffic control went down, disrupting air traffic across the nation.

The president's advisors could not agree. What was going on? Was it coincidence? Carelessness? Or was it something more sinister?

The second day, power went out in northern California and Oregon. Computerized patient records at a large Chicago hospital disappeared. Doctors and nurses in intensive care were frantic. How many patients would die as a result?

Even the most conservative of the president's advisers had to agree that this was more than bad luck or coincidence. It had to be a deliberate attack.

By the third day, the power in Miami, Minneapolis, and all of Kansas was down. Manhattan traffic lights froze, and traffic snarled. In Addis Ababa, the U.S. ambassador to Ethiopia was kidnapped. An American Airlines jet en route from New York to London was hijacked to Libya. And U.S. spy satellites that cover the Middle East went blind.

The president consulted top advisers. What should the United States do next?[3]

Nightmare

This is the nightmare that haunts the waking hours of Richard Clarke, special cybersecurity adviser to presidents George Bush, Bill Clinton, and George W. Bush. Clarke says:

> Most people don't understand. They think I'm talking about a 14-year-old hacking into their Web sites. I'm talking about people shutting down a city's electricity, shutting down 911 systems, shutting down telephone networks and transportation systems. You black out a city, people die. Black out lots of cities, lots of people die. It's as bad as being attacked by bombs.[4]

But why would anyone want to launch a cyberattack on the United States? "To extort us," Clarke said in 1999. "To intimidate us. To get us to abandon our foreign policy—'Abandon Israel or else!'"[5]

Today, no one today expects a major cyberwar. Contrary to what many have claimed, a cyberenemy will not be able to bring the country to its knees with the click of a mouse or with a few keystrokes on a laptop thousands of miles away. A devastating cyber-attack would have to be prolonged to create the kind of disruption that would bring the nation to its knees. It would require the kind of planning and long-term activity that leaves footprints, as opposed to the usual hit-and-run hacks. The cyberattackers would not be able to count on remaining anonymous or safe.

"An attack on American cyberspace is an attack on the United States," says Clarke, "just as much as a landing on New Jersey."[6] And America's enemies have learned how the nation will respond to an attack on the homeland.

Even if an all-out cyberwar is not likely, disruptions of the information infrastructure still cost money and erode public confidence. Every American has had some experience with the kind of problems that can come true when a part of the information infrastructure stops functioning:

- 2000: A computer glitch grounded planes at airports in Boston, New York, Philadelphia, and Washington, D.C., snarling plane traffic nationwide for a day.

- June 1999: Flawed input data caused the Olympic gasoline pipeline's main and back-up computers to fail. The resulting explosion killed three young people in Bellingham, Washington.

A staff sergeant and senior airman use a laptop computer to process incoming personnel. The military is as dependent on the information infrastructure as the rest of American society.

- 1998: A damaged Galaxy IV satellite blacked out pagers nationwide, interrupted radio and television broadcasts, and disrupted some bank and credit card services.

- 1991: A farmer burying a dead cow cut a fiber cable, taking down twenty-seven circuits and four of the FAA's twenty major air traffic control centers for more than five hours.

All of these glitches happened to systems owned by private industry and business. But they affected individual citizens and the government as well.

The Government: Lagging Behind

For much of American history, the federal government was at the forefront of scientific and technological innovation. In fact, the writers of the Constitution gave Congress the responsibility of promoting the progress of science and "useful arts." Often it was the military that explored new technologies in order to build bigger and better weapons.

Business and industry began to take more of the lead with the coming of electronic communications. Private industry developed and ran the telephone system. Radio and television were also run by industry, not government. Originally the Department of Defense owned the Internet, but it grew up and took off on its own. With the cyberboom of the 1990s, private industry left the federal government scrambling to catch up.

That is why the government by itself cannot protect the nation's information infrastructure from cyber-attack. Only a partnership of government, business, and average Americans—working together—can protect the national information infrastructure.

8

Cyberwar: Fiction?

In a classic children's story, an acorn falls on Chicken Little's head. Chicken Little thinks the sky must be falling, and he runs to tell the world. In the end, of course, he and his friends realize that the sky is not falling after all. Is the cybersky falling? Some experts say no.

The Satellites Are Falling—Maybe

February 1999: A band of hackers claimed to have hijacked one of Britain's Skynet 4 military communications satellites and altered its orbit. North American Aerospace Defense Command (NORAD) and other space-monitoring agencies detected the incident. The hackers demanded around $500,000 from the British government.[1] If the demand was not met, the hackers could burn up the satellite's fuel, making it useless.

How did this happen? Not just anybody can change a satellite's altitude. How did the hackers bypass encrypted command codes? How did they hack into the satellite's uplink? Did programmers create a back door in the software that controlled the satellite? Did an insider sell command information to a spy ring?[2]

In March, Britain's Ministry of Defense released a statement that no one had taken over any satellites. But some in the defense industry were not so sure. Rumor spawned rumor on the Internet: New Scotland Yard was investigating an American hacker group. No, claimed another rumor, the Russians did it. The British released another Skynet shortly after the story broke. Would it take the place of the hijacked satellite? Had the new satellite bumped the hijacked satellite to get it back into its proper orbit?[3] Was the sky falling, or was it an acorn? Someone may know the answer, but no one is talking.

So it is with the threat of cyberwar. Some say the sky is falling. Some say it is only an occasional acorn that falls on the heads of networked computer users. Can anyone know for sure?

Chicken Littles

The Chicken Littles are sure they know for sure, and they are convinced that the sky is falling. U.S. Congressman Newt Gingrich spent three years studying cyberthreats against the United States as a member of the bipartisan Hart-Rudman commission on national security. Based on this, he described the coming

In 1999, hackers claimed to have hijacked a British satellite. Whether they actually did or not is a matter of dispute. Shown above is an Echo satellite from NASA's Langley Research Center.

cyberwar in his April 2001 article, "Threats of Mass Disruption." But most of his warnings are of things that *could* happen with little evidence that they *will* happen.

Our adversaries are becoming more sophisticated, Gingrich says, and they could cause major disruptions that *could* unravel our economy, diminish our quality of life, and generally destabilize the nation. Among his warnings: "An attack on the national air traffic control systems . . . could result in widespread damage to property and infrastructure, and serious loss of life." And "airline safety could be seriously compromised if air traffic computers were hijacked by cyberterrorists."[4]

But could it really happen? Not likely, says a 1996

Senate report on cyberspace security. Federal Aviation Administration communications are the least likely to be the target of a cyberterrorist attack. They are so antiquated that modern hacking tools are useless against them.[5]

Gingrich warns: "One relatively smart hacker can cause a major economic disruption, potentially bringing some nations and markets to their knees."[6]

It is true that in the last twenty years, the number of people with computer skills has grown dramatically. But just because there are plenty of cyber-savvy individuals out there does not mean that the attacks we are likely to face are going to be as damaging as some people fear. If there are so many malicious hackers at work, why have their attacks been, by and large, fairly harmless? "The large majority of attacks demonstrate no more than script-kiddie skill level," says Tim Shimeall, a senior member of the technical staff with Carnegie Mellon University's Computer Emergency Response Team (CERT).[7] This means that most attacks are mere annoyances, pulled off by "wannabe" hackers using software they downloaded from the Internet.

There is a lot of software that can crack passwords, steal files, install malicious software in a target, or cause denial-of-service attacks. But the hacker tools available on the Internet are unlikely to cause large-scale damage. "Script kiddies are getting their clickers on more sophisticated tools, but they have little ability to do more than launch them," says John Arquilla, of the Naval Postgraduate School in California. Downloadable hacker tools reproduce past attacks. Only sophisticated hackers have the knowledge and the tools to carry out what no one has carried out before, such as widespread attacks on the electrical grid.[8]

Gingrich continues:

It is conceivable in the next 25 years that a . . . small country with cyberwarfare resources . . . will decide that it can blackmail the United States into accepting its demands by paralyzing our communications and financial systems."[9]

Not likely, says Vice Admiral Arthur K. Cebrowski, a Navy authority on cyberwar. Large-scale computer attacks would require detailed intelligence about a nation's hardware and software systems. An attacker would also have to know the habits and decision-making processes of key players. Electronic attack is not that precise.[10] Furthermore, modern computer networks are not centralized, and smart workers back up their work. That means that a single cyberattack would not be likely to disable the economy of any western country.[11]

Many possible targets of cyberattack are well guarded. Critical infrastructure systems are not sitting ducks, waiting to be taken out by a skilled and motivated attacker. Most systems have elaborate security measures in place. Critical systems often have limited connections to external networks. This makes them less susceptible to attack than more open systems. Humans are also monitoring systems more closely than they used to, which means that strange behavior is more likely to be noticed quickly. Nonhuman checks tend to be effective too: Banks back up their transactions daily and store the information offline.

Suppliers of Hype

Still, people sound the alarm. Who are they? They are government and military officials who paint terrifying scenarios but refuse to disclose "sensitive" details. They are reporters who regularly quote owners of companies that "benefit from government spending to combat the threat," says George Smith, editor of the online newsletter *Crypt*.[12] They are businesses that stand to profit from overstating the problem. They are Internet hoaxers who enjoy spreading juicy tidbits, with little regard to truth. Without serious critical thinking, it may be difficult for the average American to tell whether the sky is falling or not.

The Magic Number: 250,000

Newspapers across the country reported that there were 250,000 attacks on Pentagon computers in 1995. But the actual, verified number of intrusions during 1995 was only five hundred. The larger number was an estimate based on the number of attacks—249,500—that the Pentagon *may* have failed to detect.

And those five hundred attacks—how serious were they, really? According to Attrition.org, a computer security Web site, the "attacks" included perfectly innocent events, such as mistyped passwords at log-in and other innocent attempts to connect.[13] One computer security analyst called them the virtual equivalent of a "kid walking into the Pentagon cafeteria."[14] But "250,000 intrusions into Pentagon computers," repeated in newspapers and magazines and on television, became a fact—and a cause for fear—for many Americans.

Getting It Wrong

The media often gets the story wrong, and spreads "electronic ghost stories," in the words of George

Smith. "They get spookier with every telling." In fact, he says, media accounts are so full of hype and errors that "they are useless as a barometer of the problem."[15] The result: It is hard to be sure what to believe.

In a 1992 story, *U.S. News & World Report* claimed that the National Security Agency had planted a virus in a shipment of printers bound for Iraq shortly before Desert Storm. "Once the virus was in the system," according to unidentified sources, "each time an Iraqi technician opened a 'window' on his computer screen to access information, the contents of the screen simply vanished." The unidentified source for that story? An April Fools' joke that ran on page 39 of the April 1991 edition of *Infoworld*.[16] Oops!

Overstating the Harm

Businesses and zealous prosecutors have also been known to overstate the cost of computer intrusions. In December 1988, Robert J. Riggs ("The Prophet") cracked a BellSouth computer and downloaded a file on the 911 system. He posted it to a computer bulletin board, where Craig Neidorf ("Knight Lightning") found it and published a copy in *Phrack*, a hacker online magazine.[17] A grand jury in Lockport, Illinois, charged Riggs and Neidorf with interstate transfer of stolen property worth $79,449.[18] In reality, BellSouth sold a booklet containing the same information to the public for less than $20 per copy.[19]

How did they come up with that figure? In a letter to prosecutors, Kimberly Megahee, staff manager for security at BellSouth, stated that the stolen document was BellSouth proprietary information, not to be disclosed outside BellSouth. She attached a page itemizing the cost of producing the document. It included such expenses as the following:

- writing, formatting, and editing: $15,751

- computer software: $24,500

- computer hardware: $37,850[20]

In February 2000, denial of service attacks kept customers from browsing Yahoo!, bidding on Ebay, and trading stocks on E*Trade for a few hours. Those attacks cost American business more than a billion dollars,[21] according to experts, and President Clinton put peace negotiations in the Middle East and in Northern Ireland on hold to host an Internet security summit.

NewsFactor Network estimated the damage caused by computer viruses in 2001 at between $10 billion and $100 billion, says George Smith.[22] But is this really believable? The U.S. government estimated that the war in Afghanistan could cost $12 billion. The bombing campaign against Yugoslavia in 1999 cost $3 billion. Is it really possible that computer viruses cost more than the Afghan war or the bombing campaign in Yugoslavia?[23]

In general, estimates of damage *to* businesses are much higher than the estimates of damage caused *by* businesses. When customers suffer because of mistakes made by corporations—rather than by hackers and virus writers—estimates of damage are much, much smaller. For example, in December 2001, an AT&T mistake denied Internet service to 850,000 customers for more than a week and may have deleted their unread e-mail forever. AT&T offered no estimate of damage to customers. Instead, they called that denial of service "an inconvenience."[24]

America at Risk?

Computer expert Richard Smith asked in the year 2000: "Has there ever been an attack that was a legitimate cyber attack? Has there ever been an attack outside the United States that was politically motivated? I'm not aware of any."[25]

Wayne Madsen, a policy fellow at the Electronic Privacy Information Center, points to the most logical reason not to worry. "Who would do it?" he asks. An attack on the New York Stock Exchange, for example, would not stop at the borders of United States. It would disrupt every other economy in the world. Even terrorists would not want to see that happen. "Most terrorists move their money through the same networks," Madsen said. "They stay in hotels."[26]

Like the rest of the world, cyberattackers depend on advanced information technology. If they took down the information infrastructure, how would they communicate? How would they get their message out?[27] If cyberterrorists took down the world economic system, where would they swipe their ATM cards? If they blinded observation satellites, how would they access their global positioning system receivers and cell phones?

The September 11 hijackers, for example, relied on the Internet to communicate with each other and to organize their attack. They used the networked banking system to transfer money. For their attack to succeed, it was essential that air traffic control be operating normally.

The Real Threat

The fact is that America has already experienced many of the same kinds of attacks as the Chicken Littles warn about. Some are the result of computer viruses and small-time hackers, but most are the result of "acts of God"—storms, earthquakes, tornadoes, and floods— and acts of carelessness. Kamikaze squirrels and suicidal rodents are still a greater threat to the electrical power grid, and falling trees and farmers with backhoes are a greater threat to the communications backbone, than any cyberterrrorist.[28] Computer workers who tape passwords to their computer screens or leave sensitive information online for anyone to see are far more dangerous than hackers. Lazy programmers and systems administrators, buggy software, and poor network security are the real weapons that America has to fear.

Martin Libicki, former senior fellow at the National Defense University, agrees. "I believe we will find ways to cope with these attacks, adjust and shake them off," he said, "just as we do to natural disasters like hurricanes."[29] George Smith is more blunt. "Don't believe the hype," he says. "If there's a real war, you won't miss it."[30]

9

Civil Liberties and Cyberwar

Americans' lives may not be in danger from cyberwar, but Americans' civil liberties may be. Today some very powerful people argue that since cyberspace is new and dangerous, the government needs strong new powers to control it.

The founders of the United States of America designed the U.S. Constitution to limit the abuse of government power. But in times of national danger, the government has often ignored the Constitution and the laws of the land. In times of fear, American citizens themselves are likely to give up their civil liberties.

There will always be a tension between

78

liberty and safety. Most people will give up civil liberties for a while to ensure their safety. But once people give them up, civil liberties are often hard to get back.

Americans depend on their government to protect them from attack either by homegrown criminals or by foreign enemies. The nation's intelligence (spy) and law enforcement agencies have prevented attacks in the past and prosecuted those who have committed acts they could not prevent. But they have also often ignored the restrictions on the exercise of governmental power that the Constitution and the nation's laws demand.

Fear Factor

Science fiction author Arthur C. Clarke once wrote, "Any sufficiently advanced technology is virtually indistinguishable from magic."[1] Computer technology can cause fear that has little to do with the reality of how scary computers are. A survey in the early 1990s by Dell Computer Corporation showed that 55 percent of people harbored some fear of technology.[2] In a 1995 Gallup poll, about half of professional workers surveyed said they were resistant to trying new computer technologies. About 35 percent of them did not use a computer either at home or in the office. Even fewer subscribed to a computer on-line service such as America Online (AOL).[3] And in 1999, the word "cyberphobia," meaning a fear of computers and information technology, made its way into Webster's *New World College Dictionary*.[4] One of the things that quickly turns up when talking to people is that there is—still—a large amount of fear of computers.

People who have never experienced a virus or had a

brush with a hacker have no firsthand experience to evaluate how serious a threat these things really are. People make laws who have never sent an e-mail or surfed the World Wide Web. They believe the hype because they do not know any different.

The media feeds into the fear of cyberwar and cyberterrorism, with stories full of emotionally loaded words and exaggeration in place of hard facts. For example, in April 2001, a Chinese plane got too close

People who are comfortable using computers are less likely than those with no computer experience to be fearful and to believe negative hype about cyberattacks.

to a U.S. spy plane and crashed into the China Sea. The pilot, Wang Wei, died. Chinese hackers declared cyberwar against the United States in retaliation. From April 30 to May 7, Chinese hackers defaced Web pages. They replaced original content with pictures of Wang Wei and anti-American graffiti.

On May 8, Chinese hackers declared a truce, but it was hardly necessary. Chinese hack attacks—and American counterattacks—were neither new nor threatening. In fact, Shawn Hernan of Carnegie Mellon University's Computer Emergency Response Team Coordination Center called them "business as usual."[5]

The media did not get Hernan's message. They dubbed the "hack-fest" the "May Day War" and generated headlines like "Chinese Hacker Attacks put U.S. Sites on Notice,"[6] "US under Chinese Hack Attack,"[7] and "Is This World Cyber War I?"[8] *BusinessWeek Online* called the attacks "cyberterrorism,"[9] and Fox News called it "an All-Out Cyber War."[10]

Calling the May Day hacker contest a cyberwar—or any other kind of war—is a stretch, said Richard Stagg, security consultant for Information Risk Management. This was just the work of amateur hackers—"script kiddies looking for attention." The media said there was going to be a big war, so the kids with too much time on their hands gave them one, Stagg said.[11]

Why Not Call It War?

Why not call the May Day hacker contest a war? What is the harm? One problem is that the Constitution guarantees Americans basic civil liberties, such as freedom of speech, freedom from unreasonable search and seizure, and the equal protection under the law. However, the government has limited these freedoms during declared wars.

During the Civil War, Abraham Lincoln allowed Maryland legislators to be thrown into jail to keep them from voting for Maryland to secede from the Union. He prosecuted civilians before military tribunals. During World War I, the government threw hundreds of men and women into jails for expressing their political beliefs. During World War II, the government interned 120,000 American citizens in concentration camps because their ancestors were born in Japan. But these were real—not figurative—wars.

Many Americans believe that it takes a declaration of war from Congress for the government to take away their civil liberties. Just calling something a war is not enough. They are wrong. Neither the Korean War (1950–1953) nor the war in Vietnam (1964–1975) was a declared war.

During the Vietnam War, especially, the government spied on U.S. citizens on the basis of their political beliefs, reported a Senate Select Committee in 1976. Various governmental agencies spied on the National Association for the Advancement of Colored People (NAACP), the Conservative American Christian Action Council, the Women's Liberation Movement, the Reverend Martin Luther King, Jr., and his followers, and former presidential candidate Senator Adlai Stevenson, to just name a few. The U.S. Army created intelligence files on some one hundred thousand Americans, and the Internal Revenue Service investigated the tax returns of eleven thousand individuals based on their political associations.

The War on Drugs

Toward the end of the twentieth century, another undeclared war—the War on Drugs—led to the loss of the civil liberties of Americans accused of drug use or drug dealing. It is proper for the government to gather information on citizens during criminal prosecutions. It is also proper at times to seize property and to imprison people. But the nation's Constitution, the laws, and the courts have established rules that protect the rights of people accused of a crime.

The War on Drugs ate away at those protections. It gave law enforcement the power to snoop, sniff, survey, and detain suspects without a warrant or probable cause. They could seize property on slight evidence and not have to give it back, even with no evidence of personal guilt of the owner.[12]

The War on Drugs turned the United States into the nation with the highest percentage of prisoners in the industrialized world. It also led government leaders to propose some extreme solutions to the drug problem: beheading drug dealers,[13] shooting down planes suspected of smuggling drugs,[14] and establishing an "American Gulag" of remote prison camps for drug offenders through the Arctic Penitentiary Act.[15]

Many Americans believe that restrictions on civil rights are justified by the drug crisis and are acceptable, according to a *New York Times*/CBS poll.[16] A *Washington Post* poll showed that a majority of Americans agreed that police should be allowed to search the homes and cars of suspected drug dealers without a search warrant.[17]

The War on Terror—also an undeclared war—led to expansion of federal power to perform wiretaps on phone calls and e-mail; to conduct secret searches; and to detain immigrants considered a threat to national security.[18] The War on Terror also led to expanded powers to prosecute hackers,[19] eavesdropping on conversations between suspected terrorists and their lawyers,[20] and secret courts.[21]

Operation Sundevil

It was most likely fear and ignorance—rather than bad will—that led law enforcement to seize the publication *Phrack* and charge Craig Neidorf with stealing a $79,445 document from BellSouth. A similar explanation can probably be given for the targeting of Steve Jackson Games in what the Secret Service termed "Operation Sundevil."

Steve Jackson was a small role-playing games publisher. His company also ran the online bulletin board Illuminati—a kind of mini America Online. The board had more than 350 subscribers who played Jackson's game and sent and stored e-mail.

The Secret Service claimed the company was using its computers to publish a "manual on computer crime." Any investigation would have shown that the "manual on computer crime" was an instruction book for a computer game and that Jackson was a legitimate publisher. The Secret Service did not carry out even the most basic investigation, a federal judge later ruled. They confiscated Jackson's computers, printers, disks, and records, even though they knew that they were seizing documents intended for publication. They also knew—or should have known—that they were seizing private and public electronic communications and e-mail. The Secret Service kept the contents of Jackson's office for months. During that time, Secret Service agents read all e-mail of Illuminati subscribers without their consent.

The Secret Service exceeded its authority in two ways, the judge ruled. The First Amendment forbids the government to seize materials of publishers. And their failure to promptly return Steve Jackson's property caused economic damage to his corporation. In fact, Jackson had to lay off half his employees. The judge ordered the Secret Service to pay Steve Jackson Games more than $300,000 in damages, attorneys' fees, and court costs.[22]

Operation Sundevil caught the attention of powerful people in the fledgling computer industry. Mitch Kapor, founder of Lotus; Steve Wozniak, founder of Apple Computer; and John Gilmore of Sun Microsystems joined Wyoming rancher and computer enthusiast John Perry Barlow to found the Electronic Frontier Foundation (EFF). The purpose of the EFF is to protect freedom "where the law and technology collide."[23]

John Perry Barlow saw the Steve Jackson Games and *Phrack* cases as a threat to free speech in cyberspace. If the government could shut down *Phrack* or Steve Jackson Games because they had a stolen document on their computers, he wondered, couldn't they as easily shut down the *New York Times*, seizing its every material possession, from notepads to presses?[24] After all, in 1971, the *New York Times* published a portion of the stolen Pentagon Papers. President Richard M. Nixon tried to halt publication. Attorney General John Mitchell argued that publishing the Pentagon Papers was a threat to national security. But the Supreme Court held that the First Amendment prohibited "prior restraint" on the press. "It therefore surprises me," Georgetown professor Dorothy Denning said, "that there is any doubt that electronic publications should be accorded the same protection as printed ones."[25]

Today, the EFF continues to protect the computer community from lawmakers, law officers, and businesses that act as if cyberspace should not be protected by the same laws that protect the physical world.

Exceptions to the Bill of Rights

If there can be drug and terrorism exceptions to the Bill of Rights, can there be a computer exception, too? If there can be an exception for terrorists, can there be an exception for hackers, too? Will the U.S. government hold hackers without charging them? Will there be secret trials for hackers?

It is possible. Britain[26] and the United States have already moved to label hackers terrorists. The 2001 Anti-Terrorism Act added computer hacking to the list of federal terrorism offenses, with penalties of up to life imprisonment. The law also gave police broad new preconviction seizure powers and made it a crime to help or shelter individuals suspected of causing even minimal damage to networked computers. The law also eliminated the statute of limitations for terrorist crimes—and hacking is a terrorist crime under the law—and will apply retroactively.

Backers of the Anti-Terrorism Act argue that the bill is not aimed at teenage hackers.[27] That may be true. However, once laws are on the books, they are often used in ways their authors never intended. The intent of the law is less important that what the law says.

"Essential Liberty"

"Power exercised in secret," said former Senator William Proxmire, "especially under the cloak of national security, is doubly dangerous."[28] And it is very hard to get back civil liberties once they have been lost. During times of fear, it is a natural response to reach out for whatever will ease the fear and offer security. But as Benjamin Franklin said, "They that can give up essential liberty to obtain a little temporary safety deserve neither liberty nor safety."[29] These were not empty words. Benjamin Franklin was a traitor to the British Crown, and he faced death by hanging even as he wrote those words.

10

Defending
Cyberspace

Cyberwar may not be the threat some have made it out to be. But no one wants a cyberwar to surprise the United States the way the planes that hit the World Trade Center buildings did. It is not a bad idea to take sensible precautions.

Richard Clarke, top cybersecurity adviser to President George W. Bush, outlined his program for defending the country's computers in an interview with ZDNet News. First, he calls for training, education, and awareness. Second, he calls for industry to build better security into computer and network products. Third, he calls for everyone to demand security and to be willing to pay for it.

Training, Education, and Awareness

The government can begin with training its own employees in better computer security. "Ninety percent of the hacks on government systems occur because people haven't updated the patches on their operating systems or applications," Clarke said.[1] Other security mistakes: Employees use easy-to-guess passwords, fail to change those passwords regularly, or leave their passwords in plain sight of their computers. Many do not update antivirus software or apply security patches.

Investigators from the General Accounting Office (GAO), whose investigators regularly hack into federal computers to test their security, support Clarke. In 2001, investigators found that many agencies could not detect intrusions. They also managed to gain physical access to computers at some agencies. They walked right past security guards at federal buildings. They sat down at empty computer desks unchallenged. And they took over entire agency networks by signing on to unguarded computers as system administrator—no password required.[2] Another GAO investigation found that the National Infrastructure Protection Center, whose job it is to prevent cyberattacks, did not have enough staff to monitor the Internet twenty-four hours a day.[3]

Building in Security

The Navy missile cruiser USS *Yorktown* carries one of the most sophisticated air defense systems in the world, the AEGIS Combat System. AEGIS detects, tracks, and destroys enemy aircraft, missiles, submarines, and ships. The ship's computers control the function of all other systems on board. They evaluate threats and select, schedule, and control weapons, such as surface-to-air missiles, antisubmarine rockets, and surface-to-surface cruise missiles.

But in September 1998, a software glitch left the *Yorktown* dead in the water off the coast of Virginia. The Navy had to tow the ship back to base. It took two days of maintenance to fix the problem.

What happened? A petty officer fed bad data into the Remote Data Base Manager.[4] He tried to divide by zero, and that shut down the ship's operating system.

How could a small error take out a Navy ship? A cheap calculator does not break down every time someone tries to divide by zero, says Anthony DiGiorgio, who worked twenty-six years as a civilian engineer with the Navy's Atlantic Fleet Technical Support Center. "It seems that the computers on the *Yorktown* were not designed to tolerate such a simple failure."[5]

DiGiorgio said the flaw was in the ship's computer operating system, Microsoft Windows NT. Windows NT is proprietary software. The Navy cannot see or adjust the source code without violating its agreement with Microsoft. "Using Windows NT on a warship is similar to hoping that luck will be in our favor,"[6] DiGiorgio said. An open-source operating system is more reliable. An open-source system has code that anyone can see. A programmer could have spotted the bad data that caused the problem that took out the USS *Yorktown* and fixed it right away.

Software companies have been incredibly lax about marketing software riddled with security flaws. Microsoft, for example, released Windows 2000 with sixty-three thousand "potential known defects."[7] Some of these bugs can cause computers to crash, delete files,

In 1998, the USS Yorktown—*a missile cruiser that carries the AEGIS Combat System—was disabled when someone fed bad data into the computer, which shut down the ship's operating system. (Shown above is another ship with the AEGIS system.)*

and allow hackers to install viruses.[8] Other bugs let hackers read, modify, or delete files on users' computers.[9] Still others threaten the integrity of confidential information or make computers vulnerable to denial of service attacks.[10]

The world's most successful security intrusions— Melissa, Anna Kournikova, Love Bug, Code Red, and Nimda—have exploited weaknesses in Microsoft products, says Peter Tippet of TruSecure. The cost has been in the billions of dollars.[11] And keeping up with Microsoft's almost weekly security patches made owning Microsoft's Web server less than cost-effective.[12] Microsoft is not the only buggy software on the market, but it is the most common. Viruses that target Microsoft can infect many more computers than those that target other operating systems, such as Unix, Macintosh, or Linux.

Worms and viruses are a threat, but punishing hackers will not solve the problem of companies that rush flawed software into the hands of consumers. Digital security may require that companies pay more attention to the quality of their products, even if that means releasing new versions less often and charging more for software. However, unless the public demands better software, companies will not provide it.

Demanding Security

The government, which uses Microsoft Windows software to run almost every computer system—from those on desktops to aircraft carriers to NASA—has begun to demand better security. Infrastructure owners and operators should also demand that their vendors provide safe products. Government, business, and owners must realize that they will have to pay for increased security. If software companies do not clean up their act, then it is up to Congress to pass laws to force the issue. This is the cost of national cyber-security, after all.

Another problem is the lack of trained security experts who know how networks are built. Much of what computers do goes on behind the scenes. Most users have no idea what is causing the computer to do what it is doing. Nor do most users know if there are flaws in the software they use. People who do not understand these things cannot make smart decisions about what to do to keep their systems as safe as possible.

Computer security experts are trained to know what

is going on underneath the surface, and they do not come cheap. They command high salaries. Business can afford to pay computer security experts much better salaries than the government can. To help solve that problem, the Clinton administration suggested a Cyber Corps—information security students who would receive scholarships in exchange for working for two years in the government's Federal Cyber Services program.[13]

Honesty Is the Best Policy

Richard Clarke did not mention one of the most important strategies for defending the nation from cyberattack: being honest about the threat. An honest government is open about the threats the nation's cybernetworks face. It does not cry wolf when no danger exists. An honest press reports the situation fairly and accurately.

Brigadier General Dale Meyerrose was a lowly colonel working out of Langley Air Force Base when he received an e-mail from President Clinton. Meyerrose did not believe the e-mail was really from the president. Presidents, after all, do not write casual e-mail messages to colonels. Furthermore, the text of the e-mail contained most unpresidential name-calling.

Meyerrose ordered an investigation. Who had hijacked White House e-mail? And who was using the base's computer system behind the Air Force's back? Langley Air Force Base is the headquarters for the Air Combat Command. Air Combat Command coordinates and carries out all Air Force fighter and bomber missions worldwide. Someone who could impersonate the president could also impersonate a general and send out bogus orders.

Investigators studied the incoming e-mail for clues. They found out that the amount of traffic traveling through the network's servers to outside networks was much larger than the amount of e-mail the base itself received each day. Langley's system had become a relay point for bogus e-mail—mostly hate mail and pornography bound for America Online subscribers. Investigators worried that AOL subscribers would believe that it was really the Air Force that was sending the hate mail and porn.

Langley had to regain control of the network. But investigators did not want to shut down the e-mail system. After all, the whole base depended on it to communicate.

Tim Bass, a security consultant, helped them design a program that separated out suspicious e-mail and sent it to "jail" on another part of the server. Later, investigators could study it for more clues.

To the hackers, it seemed that their mail had disappeared down a black hole. They got mad. They said, "If you're going to block our mail, then we're going to make sure you don't get any." They flooded Langley computer systems with up to seventy-five thousand e-mail bombs per day. The e-mail server crashed. No one on the base could access their e-mail.

The Langley computer squad, the Tiger Team, worked to upgrade the e-mail system. They moved it to a faster, larger computer. They worked around the clock to turn Bass's original software into a sophisticated hacker-busting program. But the hackers were also sophisticated. They quickly figured out each Langley fix and got around it. At one point, they even used White House servers to launch e-mail bombs at Langley. The Tiger Team countered with new fixes.

The e-mail bombs continued for a month. During that time, some 80 percent of the e-mail traffic coming into the Langley system was from the attackers. The Tiger Team's software, which they named Bombshelter, directed it all into a black hole.

And then the attacks stopped. The Tiger Team and Langley Air Force Base had won the war against the hackers. They had learned something in the fighting of that war. They learned the importance of protecting their computer systems. Langley's new e-mail system no longer allowed hackers to use its servers as a relay point.[14] And thanks to the Tiger Team, the U.S. military was ready when hackers attacked NATO computer systems during the bombing of Serbia in 1999.

Government and industry and especially the media—can decrease the risk of cyberattack by being open and honest with the American people. Openness about the Langley attack helped rather than hurt. When hackers attacked NATO computers during the war in Yugoslavia, system administrators used the information the Tiger Team had gathered and published about the attacks at Langley. They used the Bombshelter software the Tiger Team developed to keep damage to NATO computers to a minimum.

Locking Doors

For Richard Clarke, cybersecurity may be as simple as locking doors. Most home owners lock their doors every night. Most car owners turn off their engines and lock the doors when they park. Those are simple acts that keep unauthorized users out of their homes and cars. Computer and Internet users who want to keep hackers out will do the same. They will "lock the doors" to their computer systems, and they will remember to lock them every day.

Someone once said that eternal vigilance is the price of liberty. In today's networked world, perhaps this should be rephrased: Eternal vigilance is the price of cybersecurity—and, therefore, national security. Individual Internet users have traditionally not bothered to learn much about the powerful tools they now have on their desktops—their computers. They have not learned what it takes to keep their computer secure. But as more and more Americans turn to superfast high-speed access lines that keep their computers connected to the Internet all the time, the odds of having their computers hijacked for evil purposes increase.

In the past, many people have looked at cyber-security as something they could never understand. And hackers would always get the upper hand anyway, so why bother? But making a computer secure is similar to driving a car safely. Computer users who "drive" their computers in Internet traffic should take some responsibility for their own safety and the safety of other computer users.

So how can computer users take responsibility to keep the Information Superhighway as safe as possible? Buying and using the latest antivirus software and firewalls is a first step. Installing and using those protections correctly is a second. Smart Internet users pay attention to security advisories and apply the patches software companies release to repair security holes as they are discovered.

After knowledge, constant vigilance is the most powerful weapon. True computer security lies in the day-to-day grind of keeping up on the most recent threats, locking doors, and fixing holes.

War Without War

Some people say that the Zapatista uprising in Mexico in 1994 was the first true cyberwar. A small group of guerrillas used information, computers, and the power of the Internet to take on the much larger and better equipped Mexican army.

Since the 1980s, the Zapatista Liberation Army had been begging the Mexican government for reforms. They wanted the Mexican government to respect native peoples, who make up 10 percent of Mexico's population. The Zapatistas wanted the government to make society and the economy more fair for the native peoples. They wanted more land to farm. They wanted more democracy. Begging was not working, so the Zapatista rebels decided to try a new plan.

New Year's Day, 1994: Some twelve thousand armed rebels occupied five towns and a city in Chiapas, Mexico's southernmost state. The uprising killed almost 150 people.

The Mexican government sent soldiers to put down the uprising. By the end of 1994, the Mexican army said that it had surrounded the Zapatistas. There appeared to be nothing for the rebels to do but surrender.

Netwar

One of the Zapatista leaders, Subcomandante Marcos, turned to the Internet. Formerly a college professor, Marcos understood that words could be more powerful than bullets. He understood that capturing headlines could be more important than capturing prisoners. He understood that "when an Indian is murdered in the forest, he makes no noise. Unless, that is, his scream is broadcast over the Internet."[1]

His laptop plugged into the cigarette lighter of his jeep,[2] Marcos put the word out that the Zapatistas had slipped out of the Mexican army's trap. The rebels, he said, had gone on to conquer dozens of villages.

This was not true. But the report of the Zapatistas shook the Mexican people's trust in their government. There was a run on the already weak peso. Pesos worth 30 U.S. cents dropped in value to about 13 cents within two months.[3] Mexico fell into recession.

Subcomandante Marcos called for everyday Mexican citizens and activists worldwide to join in a peaceful struggle for social, economic, and political change. He used the Internet to tell the world that Mexican soldiers and police were torturing and executing rebels and their families. Eyewitnesses posted firsthand reports of well-armed Mexican soldiers attacking defenseless Mayan Indians.

To the outside world, the Mexican government's response to the Zapatistas looked heavy-handed. Human-rights and indigenous-rights activists from around the world came—physically and electronically —to help the Zapatistas. Activists wanted to monitor conditions for themselves. They pushed nonviolently for access to the war zone. They demanded a cease-fire and a withdrawal of government troops. They called for the Mexican government to negotiate with the Zapatistas and to begin democratic reforms. The Mexican government moved to keep journalists and human-rights activists out of the conflict zone. But the Internet kept the light of the global media focused on Chiapas. What was once a local uprising became a global issue.[4]

Reporters worldwide picked up the news. Soon stories about the struggle and the protests began to show up on the evening news.

Public Relations War

The Zapatistas did not fight the kind of war the Mexican army would win. They would fight a new kind of war—a war of information, a cyberwar, a public relations war.

The Information Age has changed the way people fight wars. In the future, it will be easier for smaller groups to take on the power of nations. It can be enough to splash their message across the biggest billboard in the world—the Internet.

The Zapatistas would have lost a traditional war

against the much stronger Mexican army. But Subcomandante Marcos won the PR war. It was international pressure, not guns or bombs, that forced the Mexican government to stop its attacks on the Zapatistas.

War Without War

The hope was that a kind of cyberwar that depends more on getting out the story than on killing enemies would resolve problems without much bloodshed. Colonel Mike Tanksley, head of the Army infowar center at Fort Belvoir, thinks it may be possible. The

As the Zapatista Liberation Army found in Mexico in 1994, a keyboard can be more powerful than a rifle in the war over public opinion.

Internet has created a new "place" to promote ideas and causes, and people around the world have come to listen. "You can stop a war before it starts," he said.[5]

Pentagon adviser John Arquilla agrees. Today, war is about "how to win the battle of 'the story,'"[6] he says.

> These days missiles are not only tipped with warheads but with video cameras; television and radio deliver war news as it happens; and alleged eyewitness accounts of battles and massacres appear on the Internet, quickly finding their way into other media. What matters in today's combat is whose story wins.[7]

Turning to the Internet for political expression and conflict is an inevitable consequence of the Information Revolution. And it is not uncommon. It is indicative of cyberspace that a territory the size of East Timor is at the center of what has become a global issue and has attracted participants worldwide.[8]

The International Campaign to Ban Land Mines, which won the Nobel Peace Prize in 1997, turned to the Internet for support. So did the dissidents of Burma, the Tamil Tigers of Sri Lanka, and the pro-independence East Timorese of Indonesia.

In 1975, Indonesia invaded the Portuguese colony of East Timor. In an effort to force the colony to become a part of Indonesia, militias paraded through the streets of the capital city with the severed heads of East Timorese patriots on spikes.[9] They arrested, tortured, raped, or executed thousands. One third of the population of East Timor died or disappeared. The world media barely reported the tragedy.

Nobel Peace Prize winner José Ramos-Horta became East Timor's international spokesman, seeking peace for the region. He went on to fight for East Timor's independence, turning to the Internet to get the message out to the world.[10] At last, in August 1999, under the supervision of the United Nations, the East Timorese voted overwhelmingly for independence.

Now it was time to make sure Indonesia honored the results of the election. If the Indonesian government denied East Timor independence, Ramos-Horta promised, the East Timorese would fight back—in cyberspace. Hackers would sabotage Indonesia's computer networks and cause economic chaos.

Some people are not happy that previously powerless people now have access to this powerful new medium. Dino Patti Djala, a senior official of Indonesia's foreign ministry, called the threat "terrorism against democracy."[11] Angry soldiers of the militia backed by the Indonesian army left East Timor, burning whatever they could as they left.[12] But East Timor was finally free, thanks to the power of the Internet to tell the story.

12

Cyberpeace

The Palestinian lay in the bed. Noa wondered if she would live through the night. The Israeli slept not six feet away. Bushra, too, wondered if she would die before morning.

The girls did live through that night. And in the next thirty-five nights and days, they—like so many other teens from war-torn countries who attended the Seeds of Peace camp in Maine—became friends.[1] What is more, they are still friends, even though suspicion, hate, and war divide their two countries.

Teens who grow up in the Middle East carry a huge load of history on their backs every day. They learn to fear their neighbors almost from birth. They know the face of their enemy through stereotypes. For Israeli teens, any Palestinian could be a suicide bomber. For Palestinians, Israelis are the people who bulldoze their homes and force them into refugee camps.

Most of the teens would never have a chance to meet the enemy face-to-face. But Noa and Bushra did. At the Seeds of Peace camp in Maine, they found a safe place to look into each others' eyes and hearts. They took on tough topics: What is the difference between a freedom fighter and a terrorist? How can people who have hated each other for so long learn to live in peace? And the question that bitterly divides the Middle East: Who gets Jerusalem?[2]

The teens—they call themselves Seeds—did not learn to agree on the answers. They learned to agree to disagree. They learned to sympathize with their new friends' suffering. They listened to one another argue and yell. They forgave. They comforted one another when they cried. They learned to be friends.

That was the easy part. Going home was harder. At home, the borders were physical—armed soldiers and police—and psychological. Many parents were afraid of their new ideas.[3] Friends criticized them. Some said they had been brainwashed.[4] Some called them traitors.[5] Their time in Maine seemed far away. Their support system was gone.

But since 1998, the Seeds have been able to keep in touch all year round—through the Internet. They send each other e-mails every day. Sometimes they talk about recent terrorist bombings or stone-throwing riots. They check on one another to see if everyone is safe. Sometimes they argue. Other times they send words of

Through the Seeds of Peace organization, young people from different cultures meet and become friends in the United States. When they return to their home countries, they stay connected through the Internet.

reassurance and comfort. But most of the time they talk about the things that unite them—soccer, music, movies, dating, school, and family.[6]

An Israeli girl organized a chat room. The first chat ran two hours. Now the teens chat weekly. Teens from other war-torn countries—India and Pakistan; Serbia, Bosnia, and Croatia; Egypt; Jordan; and Morocco—now attend the Seeds of Peace camp and continue their friendships on the Internet. Students like Andri, a girl from Greek Cyprus, and Alp, a boy from Turkish Cyprus, who live in a land that keeps them apart with barbed wire, communicate via e-mail and instant messages.[7]

It is not only the Seeds who know that the Internet

is a force for peace. War turns on information, but so does peace—and maybe more so. Electronic access to information gives the people powers never before possible.

Openness Equals Peace

Information can stop wars before they begin if governments and their citizens will only allow that to happen. Aside from the Seeds, only a few other organizations are actively using the Internet to make peace. One is the Sandia National Laboratories. Experimenters there predicted that more information could keep disputes from turning into wars. If potential enemies could build up monitoring networks, they would not have to worry about the possibility of a surprise attack. In 1993, Sandia brought Israelis and Palestinians together for simulated "peace games."

Some people have proposed creating a global infosphere. The system would be a public resource. It would give militaries and everyday people a God's-eye view of the world in real time. Anyone could see threats anywhere in the globe. The media could publicize them. Neighbors could talk about them over the back fence. Web surfers could debate the government's response in chat rooms. With no opportunity to pull off a surprise attack, armies and terrorists would think twice about starting a war.

Cyberpeace

After the September 2001 terrorist attacks, Jawad Issa, an eighteen-year-old Palestinian from Gaza City, was attending college in Washington, D.C. He could not contact his parents in Gaza City to tell them he was safe. An Israeli girl he had met at the Seeds of Peace camp sent him an e-mail from Israel and offered to call his parents for him.[8]

That e-mail was a bright spot in a time when the fear and anger surrounding the attacks reminded Issa of life in the Middle East, where Jews and Arabs alike face threats of terrorism every day. "It was just like home," he said. "Something happens and somebody close to you dies. Any retaliation seems fair."[9]

Compared to making peace, retaliation is easy. Compared to making peace, war is easy. Cyberwar is easy. Killing people, bombing cities, and spreading terror are easier than making and keeping peace. Making peace is left to individual people. Fortunately, there is a group of young people—connected only by e-mail and memories of a summer camp in Maine—who leave camp committed to working to make peace a reality.

Chapter Notes

Chapter 1. Cyberwar

1. Jon Swartz, "Cyber Attack May Be Next, Some Worry," *USA Today*, September 13, 2001, p. 5B.

2. Jim Puzzanghera and Elise Ackerman, "U.S. Networks Run Big Risk of Cyber-Strikes, Experts Assert," San Jose *Mercury News*, September 30, 2001, <http://www0.mercurycenter.com/partners/docs/084017.htm> (October 5, 2001).

3. Jonathan Ungoed-Thomas, "How 'Datastream Cowboy' Took U.S. to the Brink of War," *The Toronto Star*, April 12, 1998, p. 1.

4. Office of the Under Secretary Of Defense For Acquisition & Technology, "Report of the Defense Science Board Task Force On Information Warfare—Defense (IW-D)," DoD96, November 1996, Washington, D.C., 20301-3140.

5. "Information Warfare," *Institute for the Advanced Study of Information Warfare*, n.d., <www.psycom/net/1war.1.html> (October 31, 2002).

6. Dan Rather and Wyatt Andrews, "Terror By Internet Becomes Virtual Reality," *CBS Evening News with Dan Rather*, January 7, 2000.

7. Matthew Campbell, "Russian Hackers Steal U.S. Weapons Secrets," *Sunday Times*, July 25, 1999, <http://www.sunday-times.co.uk/news/pages/sti/99/07/25/stifgnusa03003.html?999> (September 2, 2001).

8. Tom Gjelten, "Analysis: Cyberwarfare," *Talk of the Nation*, National Public Radio, April 23, 2001.

9. Martin Libicki, "What Is Information Warfare?" *Institute for National Strategic Studies*, August 1995, <http://www.ndu.edu/inss/actpubs/act003/a003ch01.html> (November 9, 2001).

Chapter 2. Information, Technology, and War

1. "Timeline: Life on the Internet," *PBS Online*, n.d., <http://www.pbs.org/internet/timeline/timeline-txt.html> (November 2, 2001).

2. "How Many Online?" *NUA Surveys*, 1995–2001, <http://www.nua.ie/surveys/how_many_online/world.html> (December 10, 2001).

3. Unclassified testimony of George J. Tenet, Director of CIA, delivered to Senate Committee on Governmental Affairs, June 24, 1998.

4. John Christensen, "Bracing for Guerrilla Warfare in Cyberspace," *CNN Interactive*, April 6, 1999, <http://www.cnn.com/TECH/specials/hackers/cyberterror/> (December 9, 2001).

5. Russell G. Matthews, "Another Pearl Harbor by Year 2000—This Time Online?" *Infowar.com*, February 19, 1996, <http://www.infowar.com> (October 27, 2002).

6. Matthew G. Devost, "Political Aspects of Class III Information Warfare: Global Conflict and Terrorism," Second International Conference on Information Warfare, Montreal, Canada, January 18–19, 1995, <http://www.devost.net/archives/000009.html> (October 27, 2002).

7. "B-2 Spirit," Fact Sheet, United States Air Force, Air Combat Command, Office of Public Affairs, Langley, Virginia, March 2001, <http://www.af.mil/news/factsheets/B_2_Spirit.html> (July 1, 2002).

Chapter 3. Attack of the Vandals

1. Doug Struck, "'Rites of Youth': Hacking in the '90s," *The Washington Post*, March 21, 1998, p. A15.

2. Richard Cole, "FBI Prowls for Internet Hacker," *The Topeka-Capital Journal, CJOnline*, March 8, 1998, <http://www.cjonline.com/stories/030898/tec_hacker.html> (October 30, 2002).

3. Jim Doyle, "Cloverdale Hackers Called Pranksters," *San Francisco Chronicle Online*, March 5, 1998, <http://www.sfgate.com/cgi-bin/article.cgi?file=/chronicle/archive/1998/03/05/MN56281.DTL> (August 4, 2001).

4. Linda D. Kozaryn, "Hamre Acts to Hamper Hackers," American Forces Press Service, March 18, 1988, <http://www.defenselink.mil/news/Mar1998/n03181998_9803182.html> (August 4, 2001).

5. "Pentagon Reports Cyberattack," *Wired News*, February 25, 1998, <http://www.wired.com/news/politics/0,1283,10539,00.html> (August 4, 2001).

6. Richard Power, *Tangled Web: Tales of Digital Crime from the Shadows of Cyberspace* (Indianapolis: Que, 2000), p. 83.

7. Kozaryn.

8. Andrew Quinn, "'It's Power, Dude'—Alleged Pentagon Hackers Speak Up," *Reuters*, March 10, 1998, <http://www.infobeat.com/stories/cgi/story.cgi?id=2553276707-ec8> (August 4, 2001).

9. Ibid.

10. James Glave, "ISP Homepage Hacker Taunts FBI," *Wired News*, March 4, 1998, <http://www.wired.com/news/print/0,1294,10689,00.html> (August 4, 2001).

11. Robert Uhlig, "Connected: Suspected Hackers Are Caught Out: Teenagers In Israel And California Face Charges After An International Computer Security Hunt," *The Daily Telegraph*, March 26, 1998, p. 4.

12. James Glave, "Hacker Raises Stakes in DOD Attacks," *Wired News*, March 5, 1998, <http://www.wired.com/news/technology/0,1282,10730,00.html> (October 27, 2002). 20. Kozaryn.

13. Kozaryn.

Chapter 4. Cyberintelligence

1. Anthony Kimery, "The Russians Are Coming! Oh Wait, They're Already Here," *Military Information Technology Online*, n.d., <http://www.mit-kmi.com/Archives/3_5_MIT/3_5_Art1.cfm> (August 7, 2001).

2. Ted Bridis, "Russian Hackers Quietly Invade U.S.," *Wall Street Journal Europe*, June 26, 2001, <http://www.infowar.com/hacker/01/hack_080301b_j.shtml> (August 7, 2001).

3. Ibid.

4. Robert X. Cringely, "Let Them Eat Borscht," *I, Cringely: The Pulpit*, PBS, November 4, 1999, <http:// www.pbs.org/cringely/pulpit/pulpit19991104.html> (September 2, 2001).

5. Bridis.

6. Vernon Loeb, "NSA Adviser Says Cyber-Assaults On Pentagon Persist With Few Clues," *The Washington Post*, May 7, 2001, p. A2.

7. Bob Drogin, "Hackers Hit Pentagon Computers," *The Dallas Morning News*, October 7, 1999, p. 1A.

8. Kimery.

9. Ruth Alvey, "Russian Hackers For Hire—The Rise Of The E-Mercenary," *Jane's Intelligence Review*, July 2001, <http://www.infowar.com/hacker/01/hack_080301a_j.shtml> (August 7, 2001).

10. Loeb.

11. James Adams, "Computer Security," Congressional Testimony, March 9, 2000.

12. Peter Graff, "Russia Denies U.S. Hack Attacks," *ZDNet News*, October 7, 1999, <http://www.zdnet.com/filters/printerfriendly/0,6061,2349412-2,00.html> (October 27, 2002).

13. Philip Elmer-DeWitt, "A Bold Raid on Computer Security," *Time*, May 2, 1988, p. 58.

14. James S. Kunen and S. Avery Brown, "Astronomer Cliff Stoll Stars in the Espionage Game, But for Him Spying Doesn't Really Compute," *People*, December 11, 1989, p. 118.

15. "FBI Haunted by West German Hackers," *THE SYNDICATE REPORT Information Transmittal*, June 13, 1989, <http://www.etext.org/CuD/Synd/synd-23> (October 27, 2002).

16. Jay Peterzell, "Spying and Sabotage by Computer," *Time*, March 20, 1989, p. 25.

17. Alvey.

18. Drogin.

19. Lisa Burgess, "Pentagon's policy change on disposal of computers is good news for schools," *Stars and Stripes*, <http://ww2.pstripes.osd.mil/01/jun01/ed060901l.html> (October 27, 2002).

20. Bob Brewin and Daniel Verton, "Cyberattacks Spur Talk of Third DOD Network," *CNN.com*, June 22, 1999, <http://www.cnn.com/TECH/computing/9906/22/dodattack.idg/> (June 16, 2001)

21. H. Keith Melton, "Spies in the Digital Age," *CNN.com*, 1998, <http://www.cnn.com/SPECIALS/cold.war/experience/spies/melton.essay/> (November 6, 2001).

Chapter 5. Taking Down the Digital Economy

1. Sam Costello, "FBI Warns Cybercrime Is on the Rise," *PCWorld*, April 8, 2002, <www.pcworld.com/news/article/0,aid,93263,00.asp> (July 1, 2002).

2. Richard Power, *Tangled Web: Tales of Digital Crime from the Shadow of Cyberspace* (Indianapolis: Que, 2000), p. 98.

3. Philip Jacobson, "Focus: Crime in the Cyber Age," *The Sunday Telegraph*, October 19, 1997, p. 29.

4. Ibid.

5. Dan Kuehl, "Cyber Threats and the US Economy," Statement Before the Joint Economic Committee of the U.S. Congress, February 23, 2000, <http://www.ndu.edu/irmc/publications/congress2.htm> (September 24, 2001).

6. Dave Murphy, "Recent 'Denial of Service' Attacks Cost $1.2 Billion," *Insider Reports*, April 11, 2000, <http://www.insiderreports.com/storypage.asp_Q_ChanID_E_WB_A_StoryID_E_20000526> (November 17, 2001).

7. "Hackers Disrupt the Business of Several Major Web Sites," *CBS Evening News with Dan Rather*, February 9, 2000.

8. Deborah Solomon and Kevin Johnson, "FBI Launches Cyberhunt," *USA Today*, February 10, 2000, p. 1A.

9. Fred Cohen, "Economic Cyber Threats," Testimony before the Joint Economic Committee of the U.S. Congress, February 23, 2000.

10. Amey Stone, "Why Internet Security Stocks Could Be a Safe Play," *BusinessWeek Online*, February 11, 2000, <http://www.businessweek.com/bwdaily/dnflash/feb2000/sw00211.htm> (October 28, 2002).

11. "Judges, Hackers, Viruses Grab Headlines in Crazy 2000 E-Commerce Lost Its Appeal in 2000," *The Toronto Star*, January 1, 2001, p. A1.

12. Richard Clayton, "Extracting a 3DES key from an IBM," n.d., <http://www.cl.cam.ac.uk/~rnc1/descrack/ index.html> (November 17, 2001).

13. James Middleton and Andy McCue, "Students Hack for PIN Money," *Computing*, September 11, 2001, <http://www.computing.co.uk/News/1126764> (November 17, 2001).

14. Tim McDonald, "Report: Year's Hack Attacks To Cost $1.6 Trillion," *E-Commerce Times*, July 11, 2000, <http://www.ecommercetimes.com/perl/story/3741.html> (November 17, 2001).

15. Paul Festa and Joe Wilcox, "Experts Estimate Damages in the Billions for Bug," *CNET News.com*, May 5, 2000, <http://news.cnet.com/news/0-1003-200-1814907.html> (November 17, 2001).

16. "The Love Bug," *NewsHour with Jim Lehrer*, PBS Online, May 5, 2000, <http://www.pbs.org/newshour/bb/cyberspace/jan-june00/lovebug_5-5.html> (May 15, 2000).

17. Ibid.

18. Ibid.

Chapter 6. Cyberterrorism

1. Mark M. Pollitt, "Cyberterrorism: Fact or Fancy?" *Proceedings of the 20th National Information Systems Security Conference*, October 1997, <http://www.cosc.georgetown.edu/~denning/infosec/pollitt.html> (September 7, 2001).

2. Industry Group 91, "Terror Can Be Just a Computer Away," *Regulatory Intelligence Data*, February 6, 1998.

3. Pollitt.

4. Arnaud de Borchgrave, Testimony before the House Committee on International Relations, International Organized Crime and Global Terrorism, October 1, 1997.

5. Barry C. Collin, "The Future of CyberTerrorism: Where the Physical and Virtual Worlds Converge," 11th Annual International Symposium on Criminal Justice Issues, n.d., <http://afgen.com/terrorism1.html> (October 31, 2002.

6. "Cyberterrorism Attacks Rise 50%," *Internet and Technology News, News Archives, Australian Cybermalls*, May 7, 2001, <http://ausmall.com.au/acnarch/acnews63.htm#010507> (September 9, 2001).

7. "Internet Terrorism at St. Petersburg's School," *Pravda*, February 19, 2001, <http://english.pravda.ru/main/2001/02/19/2582.html> (September 9, 2001).

8. "Teen-Ager at Center of Internet Terrorism Probe," *San Francisco Chronicle*, January 11, 2001, <http://www.sfgate.com/cgi-bin/article.cgi?file=/news/archive/2001/01/11/state1428ESTO164.DTL&type=tech_article> (September 9, 2001).

9. Jim Miklaszewski and Robert Windrem, "Pentagon and Hackers in 'Cyberwar,'" *MSNBC*, March 5, 1999, <http://www.zdnet.com/zdnn/stories/news/0,4586,2220773,00.html> (September 11, 2001).

10. "Work Together to Stop DoS Attacks," *InternetWeek.com*, February 6, 2001, <http://www.internetweek.com/columns01/edit020601.htm> (December 9, 2001).

11. Garry Barker, "Internet Terrorism Escalates The New Info-War," *The Age*, July 13, 1999, <http://www.theage.com.au/daily/990713/education/ed3.html> (September 9, 2001).

12. David Noack, "Banana Rumor Called 'Internet Terrorism': E-mail Claims Fruit Spread Flesh-Eating Bacteria," *APBnews.com*, February 25, 2000, <http://www.apbnews.com:80/newscenter/internetcrime/2000/02/25/bananas0225%5F01.html> (September 9, 2001).

13. Dorothy E. Denning, "Cyberterrorism," Testimony before the Special Oversight Panel on Terrorism Committee on Armed Services, U.S. House of Representatives, May 23, 2000, <http://www.cs.georgetown.edu/~denning/infosec/cyberterror.html> (September 7, 2001).

14. Caroline Benner, "The Phantom Cyber-Threat," *Salon.com*, April 4, 2001, <http://www.salon.com/tech/feature/2001/04/04/cyberterrorism/index.html> (November 30, 2001).

15. John Arquilla, David Ronfeldt, and Michele Zanini, "Networks, Netwar, and Information-Age Terrorism," in Ian O. Lesser, Bruce Hoffman, John Arquilla, David Ronfeldt, Michele Zanini, and Brian Michael Jenkins, *Countering the New Terrorism*, RAND, 1999, <http://www.rand.org/publications/MR/MR989/MR989.chapt3.pdf> (December 9, 2001).

16. Patrick McMahon, "Anti-Abortion Site Kicked Off the Web," *USA Today*, February 8, 1999, <http://www.usatoday.com/life/cyber/tech/cte338.htm> (November 27, 2001).

17. Michele Zanini and Sean J. A. Edwards, "The Networking of Terror in the Information Age," in John Arquilla and David Ronfeldt, eds., *Networks and Netwars: The Future of Terror, Crime, and Militancy*, <http://www.rand.org/publications/MR/MR1382/MR1382.ch2.pdf> (October 28, 2002).

18. *CIA World Factbook* (Washington, D.C.: Central Intelligence Agency, 1997), UM-St. Louis Libraries Edition, derived and modified by Raleigh Muns, April 20, 1998, <http://www.odci.gov/cia/publications/factbook/index.html> (July 2, 2002).

19. Sam Handlin, "Experts Say Osama's Men Used Encrypted Messages on the Internet to Communicate," *Court TV*, September 21, 2001, <http://www.courttv.com/assault_on_america/0920_cyber_ctv.html> (October 5, 2001).

20. Ibid.

21. Bill Nelson, Rodney Choi, Michael Iacobucci, Mark Mitchell, and Greg Gagnon, "Cyberterror: Prospects and Implications," Naval Postgraduate School, Monterey, Calif., December 1999, <http://www.ntis.gov/search/product.asp?ABBR=ADA393147&starDB=GRAHIST> (October 28, 2002).

22. Denning.

23. Dorothy E. Denning, "Activism, Hacktivism, and Cyberterrorism: The Internet as a Tool for Influencing Foreign Policy," Internet and International Systems: Information Technology and American Foreign Policy Decisionmaking Workshop, Georgetown University, <http://www.nautilus.org/info-policy/workshop/papers/denning.html> (September 3, 2001).

Chapter 7. Sum of All Fears: Infrastructure Warfare

1. Neil Munro, "Fear of an Electronic Pearl Harbor," *Washington Post*, July 16, 1995, p. C3.

2. Ibid.

3. Robert H. Anderson and Anthony C. Hearn, "An Exploration of Cyberspace Security R&D Investment Strategies for DARPA: "The Day After . . . in Cyberspace II," *RAND*, <http://www.rand.org/publications/MR/MR797/appb.html> (October 28, 2002).

4. Tim Weiner, "The Man Who Protects America From Terrorism," *New York Times*, February 1, 1999, p. A1.

5. Ibid.

6. Ibid.

Chapter 8. Cyberwar: Fiction?

1. Michael Buonagurio, "A Final Look at the UK Satellite Hack," *AntiOnline*, March 31, 1999, <http://www. AntiOnline.com/cgi-bin/News?type=antionline&date= 03-29-1999&story=satup.news> (April 5, 2000).

2. Michael Buonagurio, "Hackers Take Control of Satellite," *AntiOnline*, March 1, 1999, <http://www. AntiOnline.com/cgi-bin/News?type=antionline&date=03-01-1999&story=satcl. news> (April 4, 2000).

3. Michael Buonagurio, "The Satellite Hack Is It or Isn't It?" *AntiOnline*, March 2, 1999, <http://www.AntiOnline. com/cgi-bin/News?type=antionline&date=03-01-1999&story=sat2.news> (April 4, 2000).

4. Newt Gingrich, "Threats of Mass Disruption: A Cyber Pearl Harbor Is Not a Question of If, But When," *Information Security*, April 2001, <http://www.infosecuritymag.com/ articles/april01/columns_security_persp.shtml> (November 14, 2001).

5. Gary H. Anthes, "Feds Turn Blind Eye to Systems Security," *ComputerWorld*, June 17, 1996, p. 73.

6. Gingrich.

7. Caroline Benner, "The Phantom Cyber-Threat," *Salon.com*, April 4, 2001, <http://www.salon.com/tech/ feature/2001/04/04/cyberterrorism/index.html> (November 30, 2001).

8. Ibid.

9. Gingrich.

10. Bradley Graham, "Cyberwar: A New Weapon Awaits a Set of Rules: Military, Spy Agencies Struggle to Define Computers' Place in U.S. Arsenal," *The Washington Post*, July 8, 1998, p. A1.

11. "Select Enemy. Delete," *The Economist*, March 8, 1997, p. 21. Available online at Study Group on the Information Revolution and World Politics, Carnegie Endowment for International Peace, <http://www.ceip.org/infostudygroup/economist.html> (December 9, 2001).

12. George Smith, "An Electronic Pearl Harbor? Not Likely," *Issues in Science and Technology Online*, Fall 1998, <http://205.130.85.236/issues/15.1/smith.htm> (October 27, 2002).

13. "DOD 250K Figure Is Bunk," Security Scene Errata, *Attrition.org*, n.d., <http://www.attrition.org/errata/250k.html> (November 19, 2001).

14. Smith.

15. Ibid.

16. "Urban Legend: The U.S. government planted a virus (or homing beacon) in Iraqi military computers during the Gulf War," *Vmyths.com—Truth about Virus Myths and Hoaxes*, n.d., <http://iwsun5.infoworld.com/servlet/search?q=gulf+war+hoax&r=iwnews&s=0&t=10> (October 27, 2002).

17. John Perry Barlow, "Crime and Puzzlement," *Electronic Frontier Foundation*, June 8, 1990, <http://www.eff.org/Misc/Publications/John_Perry_Barlow/HTML/crime_and_puzzlement_1.html (December 2, 2001).

18. *U.S. District Court Northern District Of Illinois, Eastern Division, United States Of America*, v. *Robert J. Riggs, also known as Prophet, and Craig Neidorf, also known as Knight Lightning*, April 1987, <http://www.eff.org/Legal/Cases/SJG/Phrack_Neidorf_Riggs/neidorf_riggs.indictment> (December 2, 2001).

19. David Gans and R.U. Sirius, "Civilizing the Electronic Frontier: An Interview with Mitch Kapor and John Barlow of the Electronic Frontier Foundation," *Mondo 2000,* Winter 1991, pp. 45–49, available online at <http://www.strano.net/snhtml/ipertest/metanet/txt0/inte.htm> (December 2, 2001).

20. "Why the Bell South E911 Document Cost $79,000 to Produce," *Computer Underground Digest*, September 14, 1991, <http://venus.soci.niu.edu/~cudigest/CUDS3/cud333.txt> (December 2, 2001).

21. Patrick Neighly, "Meet the Hackers," *America's Network*, June 1, 2000, <http://www.findarticles.com/cf_dls/mODUJ/ 9_104/63539801/p1/article.jhtml> (October 27, 2002).

22. George Smith, "Dollar Diddling and the Billion-Dollar Viruses," *Crypt*, April 29, 2002, <http://online.securityfocus. com/columnists/78> (June 22, 2002).

23. Ibid.

24. Amy Reinink, "71,000 lose 'Net access in Colorado," *The Denver Post*, December 2, 2001, p. 1A.

25. "Clinton Wants Network Protections, but Critics Wary," *CNN.com*, January 7, 2000, <http://cnn.com/ 2000/TECH/ computing/01/07/clinton.security.02/index.html>(January 20, 2000).

26. Will Rodger, "Cyberwar: Proper Vigilance or Paranoia?" *Inter@ctive Week*, October 4, 1998, <http://cma.zdnet.com/ texis/techinfobase/techinfobase/+Twq_qr+W69+sW/zdisplay. html> (October 27, 2002.)

27. John Arquilla, David Ronfeldt, and Michele Zanini, "Networks, Netwar, and Information-Age Terrorism," in Ian O. Lesser, Bruce Hoffman, John Arquilla, David Ronfeldt, Michele Zanini, and Brian Michael Jenkins, *Countering the New Terrorism*, RAND, 1999, <http://www.rand.org/publications/ MR/MR989/MR989.chapt3.pdf> (December 9, 2001).

28. Peter G. Neumann, "Illustrative Risks to the Public in the Use of Computer Systems and Related Technology," *SRI International*, November 1, 1999, <ftp://unix.sri.com/risks/ illustrative.html> (January 21, 2000).

29. Steve Lohr, "Stakes Raised in Cyber-sabotage," *New York Times*, October 29, 1996, <http://www.datasync.com/ ~sotmesc/news/iwar.txt> (July 1, 2002).

30. "'Electronic Pearl Harbor' and You Missed It . . . Again," *Crypt*, March 3–10, 1999, <http://www.soci.niu.edu/~crypt/ other/modolts2.htm> (December 9, 2001).

Chapter 9. Civil Liberties and Cyberwar

1. Arthur C. Clarke, *Profiles of the Future: An Inquiry into the Limits of the Possible* (New York: Holt, Rinehart, and Winston, 1984), p. 36.

2. K. Hogan, "Technophobia," *Forbes*, ASAP Supplement, February 28, 1994, p. 116.

3. Elisa Williams, "Many Fear Computers, Poll Finds," *St. Louis Post-Dispatch*, February 1, 1995, p. 5C.

4. Lance Carden, "How the 'Cyber' Story Is Shifting," *The Christian Science Monitor*, March 30, 2000, p. 22.

5. Sam Costello, "U.S.-China 'Cyberwar' Fires Blanks," *CNN.com*, May 11, 2001, <http://www.cnn.com/2001/TECH/internet/05/11/china.cyberwar.idg/> (November 18, 2001).

6. Don Melvin, "Chinese Hacker Attacks Put U.S. Sites on Notice," *The Atlanta Constitution*, May 4, 2001, p. B1.

7. Mark Gregory, "US under Chinese Hack Attack," April 30, 2001, *BBC News*, <http://news.bbc.co.uk/hi/english/world/americas/newsid_1305000/1305755.stm> (November 18, 2001).

8. Michelle Delio, "Is This World Cyber War I?" *Wired News*, May 1, 2001, <http://www.wired.com/news/politics/0,1283,43443,00.html> (November 18, 2001).

9. Mike France, "Red Alert over Digital Warfare on the Net," *BusinessWeek Online*, April 30, 2001, <http://www.businessweek.com/technology/content/apr2001/tc20010430_553.htm> (November 18, 2001).

10. Robin Wallace, "It's an All-Out Cyber War as U.S. Hackers Fight Back at China," *FoxNews.com*, May 01, 2001, <http://www.foxnews.com/story/0,2933,19337,00.html> (November 18, 2001).

11. Will Knight, "Experts Question US vs China 'Cyberwar'," *ZDNet UK*, May 4, 2001, <http://news.zdnet.co.uk/story/0,,s2086036,00.html> (November 18, 2001).

12. H. Jane Lehman, "Expanded War on Drugs May Threaten Landlords," *Washington Post*, November 17, 1990, p. E1; Michael Isikoff, "Drug Raids Net Much Valuable Property—and Legal Uproar," *Washington Post*, April 1, 1991, p. A1.

13. *The Larry King Show*, June 15, 1989 (Cable News Network broadcast), quoted in "Crackmire," *The New Republic*, September 11, 1989, p. 7.

14. John Angell, "The National Drug Strategy: Escalation of the War on Drugs," *Alaska Justice Forum*, <http://www.uaa.alaska.edu/just/forum/f063fa89/adrugwar.html> (November 18, 2001).

15. American Civil Liberties Union, letter regarding the War on Drugs, *Unreasonable.org*, n.d., <http://unreasonable.org/drug_policy/war-on-drugs-aclu.html> (November 18, 2001).

16. Richard Berke, "Poll Finds Most in U.S. Back Bush Strategy on Drugs," *New York Times*, September 12, 1989, p. B8.

17. Richard Morin, "Many in Poll Say Bush Plan Is Not Stringent Enough," *Washington Post*, September 8, 1989, p. A1.

18. Manuel Perez-Rivas, "Anti-Terrorism Proposals Worry Civil Libertarians," *CNN.com*, September 25, 2001, <http://www.cnn.com/2001/US/09/25/inv.civil.liberties/> (November 18, 2001).

19. "Summary and Analysis of Key Sections of USA Patriot Act of 2001," *Center for Democracy and Technology*, n.d., <http://www.cdt.org/security/011031summary.shtml> (October 26, 2002).

20. Andrew Gumbel, "Suspects To Face Secret Trials In Military Courts," *Independent News*, November 15, 2001, <http://news.independent.co.uk/world/asia_china/story.jsp?story=105026> (November 18, 2001).

21. Jonathan Turley, "Bush's Secret Court: Legal System in a Burka," *LATimes.com*, November 15, 2001, <http://www.latimes.com/news/nationworld/nation/la-111501turley.story> (December 9, 2001).

22. Judge's decision in *Steve Jackson Games, Inc. v. U.S. Secret Service*, U.S. District Court, Austin, Texas, Division, n.d., <http://www.sjgames.com/SS/decision-text.html> (December 3, 2001).

23. "About EFF: General Information About the Electronic Frontier Foundation," *Electronic Frontier Foundation*, n.d., <http://www.eff.org/abouteff.html#history> (October 25, 2002).

24. John Perry Barlow, "Crime and Puzzlement," *Electronic Frontier Foundation*, June 8, 1990, <http://www.eff.org/Misc/Publications/John_Perry_Barlow/HTML/crime_and_puzzlement_1.html> (December 2, 2001).

25. Dorothy E. Denning, "The United States vs. Craig Neidorf: A Debate on Electronic Publishing, Constitutional Rights And Hacking," *Communications of the ACM*, March 1991, p. 24. Available online from The Electronic Frontier Foundation at <http://www.eff.org/Net_culture/Hackers/us_v_craig_neidoff.article> (December 2, 2001).

26. Will Knight, "Crackdown: Are Hackers Terrorists?" *ZDNet UK*, February 20, 2001, <http://www.zdnet.com/zdnn/stories/news/0,4586,2687991,00.html> (November 18, 2001).

27. Alfred Hermida, "Hackers 'Branded as Terrorists,'" *BBC News Online*, September 28, 2001, <http://news.bbc.co.uk/hi/english/sci/tech/newsid_1568000/1568302.stm> (December 9, 2001).

28. Arianna Huffington, "What Is Washington Trying to Hide?" *Salon.com*, May 10, 2001, <http://www.salon.com/news/feature/2001/05/10/drug_war/> (November 18, 2001).

29. Benjamin Franklin, *Historical Review of Pennsylvania*, 1759, in Justin Kaplan, ed., *Bartlett's Familiar Quotations*, 16th ed. (Boston: Little, Brown & Co., 1992), p. 310.

Chapter 10. Defending Cyberspace

1. Robert Lemos, "Defending America against Cyberterrorism," *ZDNet News*, November 12, 2001, <http://zdnet.com.com/2100-1105-531071.html> (May 23, 2002).

2. Robert O'Harrow, Jr., "Key U.S. Computer Systems Called Vulnerable to Attack," *Washington Post*, September 27, 2001, p. A6.

3. Ibid.

4. Gregory Slabodkin, "Navy: Calibration flaw crashed Yorktown LAN," *GCN*, November 9, 1998, <http://www.gcn.com/archives/gcn/1998/november9/6.htm> (July 29, 2001).

5. Anthony DiGiorgio, "The Smart Ship Is Not Enough," *Proceedings*, U.S. Naval Institute, June 1998, <http://www.usni.org/Proceedings/digiorgio.htm> (December 9, 2001).

6. Mary Jo Foley, "Somebody Call an Exterminator," *ZDNet Tech Update*, February 11, 2000, <http://pqasb.pqarchiver.com/proceedings/index.html> (October 27, 2002).

7. Ibid.

8. Nick Wingfield and Alex Lash, "Microsoft Security Flaws Run Deep," *CNET News.com*, March 6, 1997, <http://news.cnet.com/news/0-1003-201-317126-0.html> (May 5, 2001).

9. Sam Costello, "Microsoft Fixes Security Flaws in Media Player," *CNN.com*, May 25, 2001, <http://www.cnn.com/2001/TECH/ptech/05/25/ms.security.flaw.idg/index.html> (August 5, 2001).

10. Sam Costello, "Microsoft Plugs Telnet Holes in Windows 2000," *CNN.com*, June 13, 2001, <http://www.cnn.com/2001/TECH/internet/06/13/ms.plugs.holes.idg/index.html> (August 5, 2001).

11. David Berlind, "Is Microsoft Liable?" *ZDNet Tech Update*, September 19, 2001, <http://techupdate.zdnet.com/techupdate/stories/main/0,14179,2813470,00.html> (November 18, 2001).

12. John Pescatore, "Nimda: Another Worm, More Patches," *ZDNet News*, September 21, 2001, <http://zdnet.com.com/2100-1107-530741.html> (October 27, 2002).

13. Jim Landers, "In Cyber Wars, Uncle Sam Wants Youth," *The Dallas Morning News*, September 09, 1999, p. 1A.

14. Frank Vizard, "Waging War.Com," *Popular Science*, July 1999, pp. 82–84.

Chapter 11. War Without War

1. Antonio Lopez, "Twenty Days of Resistance and Solidarity in Mexican Cyberspace," n.d., <http://www.swcp.com/~eltiki/homic_page/articles/netwar.html> (August 1, 2001).

2. "The Ties that Bind," *The Economist*, June 10, 1999, p. D18.

3. Belinda Fuller and Ryratana Suwanraks, eds., "Mexico 1994 versus Thailand 1997," *TDRI Quarterly Review*, September 1997, <http://www.info.tdri.or.th/library/quarterly/text/s97_2.htm> (November 14, 2001).

4. David Ronfeldt, John Arquilla, Graham E. Fuller, and Melissa Fuller, "The Zapatista 'Social Netwar' in Mexico," *RAND*, 1998, <http://www.rand.org/publications/MR/MR994/sum.pdf/> (January 29, 2000).

5. Neil Munro, "Fear of an Electronic Pearl Harbor," *Washington Post*, July 16, 1995, p. C3.

6. Michelle L. Hankins, "Propaganda War Reaches Global Audience to Evoke International Activity," *Signal Magazine*, July 1999, <http://www.us.net/signal/Archive/July99/social-july.html> (August 1, 2001).

7. Tim McGirk, "Wired For Warfare," *Time*, October 11, 1999, p. 5.

8. Jules Bell, "East Timor Cyberwar on New Global Battlefield: The Web," *The Jakarta Post*, August 27, 1999, p. 1A.

9. Oscar Romero, "An Appeal on Behalf of East Timor," *JustPeace*, June 13, 1999, <www.justpeace.org/easttimor.htm> (June 28, 2002).

10. Bell.

11. Ibid.

12. Keith B. Richburg, "As Force Moves West, Dili Burns," *The Washington Post*, October 2, 1999, p. A18.

Chapter 12. Cyberpeace

1. Lee Michael Katz, "Summer Camp Cuts Away the Barbed Wire," *USA Today*, August 4, 1998, <http://www.seedsofpeace. org/details.cfm?id=55&section=Press%2C%20Speeches%2C% 20Links> (December 9, 2001).

2. Matthew Hay Brown, "From Seeds of Peace, Understanding Grows," *The Hartford Courant*, August 30, 1999, <http://www.seedsofpeace.org/details.cfm?id=51&section= Press%2C%20Speeches%2C%20Links> (December 9, 2001).

3. Caryle Murphy, "There's Mideast Peace in the Wilds of Maine," *The Washington Post*, August 22, 1997, <http:// www.seedsofpeace.org/details.cfm?id=57&section=Press%2C% 20Speeches%2C%20Links> (December 9, 2001).

4. Cindy Rodriguez, "Sowing Peace," *Boston Sunday Globe*, August 15, 1999, <http://www.seedsofpeace.org/details. cfm?id=53&section=Press%2C%20Speeches%2C%20Links> (December 9, 2001).

5. Ira Berkow, "Camp Tries Teamwork to Ease Tension in Middle East," *New York Times*, August 1, 2002, <http://www. seedsofpeace.org/details.cfm?id=218&section=Press%2C%20 Speeches%2C%20Links> (October 27, 2002).

6. Ibid.

7. Katz.

8. Mary K. Feeney, "For Peace Campers, Terrorism Is Familiar," *The Hartford Courant*, September 22, 2001, <http:// www.seedsofpeace.org/details.cfm?id=155&section=News> (October 5, 2001).

9. Ibid.

Glossary

ARPANET—The ancestor of the global Internet, ARPANET was a large wide-area network that the U.S. Defense Advanced Research Project Agency (ARPA) established in 1969 to link government, universities, and research centers.

back door—A hole in the security of a system that the programmers leave in deliberately. After breaking into systems, crackers also leave a hole through which they can get back into the system whenever they want.

cracker—A criminal computer programmer who maliciously breaks into computers or networks, often stealing information or crashing the network.

critical infrastructure—The foundation on which modern industrial societies are based, including telecommunications, energy, banking and finance, water systems, government operations, and emergency services.

cyberattack—An attack on, or by means of, information systems or computer networks.

cyberterrorism—A criminal act carried out through computers that causes violence, death, or destruction and creates terror to coerce a government to change its policies.

distributed denial of service (DDoS) attack—The flooding of a computer system or network with so much traffic that other people cannot access the system or network.

firewall—A network barrier designed to keep out crackers.

hacker—A talented computer programmer who enjoys finding out what computers can do and solving problems. True hackers do not carry out illegal activity.

infowar—Making war by means of viruses and other cyberweapons.

script kiddie—A technically unsophisticated cracker who uses programs available on the Internet to look for weaknesses in networks so that they can gain root access to a system.

sniffer program—A program that monitors all traffic on a network. Hackers often install sniffers to capture passwords.

supercomputer—A very fast, powerful computer designed to perform specific complex tasks very rapidly.

Further Reading

Books

De Angelis, Gina, and B. Marvis. *Cyber Crimes (Crime, Justice, and Punishment)*. New York: Chelsea House, 1999.

Godwin, Mike. *Cyber Rights: Defending Free Speech in the Digital Age*. New York: Crown, 1998.

Kroen, William C. *Hackers No More*. New York: Random House, 1994.

Mendell, Ronald. *Investigating Computer Crime*. Springfield, Ill.: Charles C. Thomas, Publisher, 1998.

Parker, Donn B. *Fighting Computer Crime: A New Framework for Protecting Information*. New York: John Wiley & Sons, 1998.

Probert, Ian. *Internet Spy*. New York: Houghton Mifflin, 1996.

Internet Addresses

Information Warfare and Information Security on the Web
<http://www.fas.org/irp/wwwinfo.html>

Institute for the Advanced Study of Information Warfare
<http://www.psycom.net/iwar.html>

Seeds of Peace
<http://www.seedsofpeace.org>

Index